# The

# Valley

# Of Death

On the night of
November 6, 1977,
the lives of several
hundred people were
changed forever
when a wall of water
poured over the
highest waterfall
east of the
Mississippi River.

Water dropped
one hundred
eighty-six feet
onto automobile size
boulders,
then careened
downstream
fifty-five feet
high traveling
one hundred-ten
miles per hour.

It raged through
a college campus,
taking everything
in its path,
to Lake Hartwell,
twenty miles away.

I was there.
I was a victim.
I am a survivor.

I lived in what I thought was
*The Garden of Eden*;
But, I lived *through* what became
*The Valley of Death.*

# The Valley Of Death
# By R. Douglas Veer

Changed Lives Publishing, LLC

2018

First Printing: 2018
ISBN-13: 978-1-7323243-1-2
Library of Congress Control Number:
2018954006

Cover Design: K. Veer
Front Cover Photo: Pete Windus
Back Cover Photo: The Dessert Engineer

\* \* \* \* \* \* \*

Book Ordering: Amazon.com
Booking Information, please contact:
Doug@DougVeer.com or
Kathy@KathyVeer.com

Changed Lives Publishing, LLC
Region of Augusta, Georgia

# DEDICATION

I dedicate this book to all of you
who lost loved ones that night,
and to those who actually walked
that valley with me.

# FORWARD

I must say,
I would be ashamed of myself
if I didn't tell you why this book is in print.

First, it was very difficult to write
because of having to wade through memories
of the pain and fear of that terrible night;
it brought all those emotions back to the present
and it became so draining that I wanted to give up.
At one point, I actually deleted the entire writing.

Second, I would like to say to my children
whom I love with all my heart:
"Thank you for always being here for me."
The pain of dealing with those emotions again
caused me to shed a lot of fresh tears.
But, thinking of you encouraged me
to continue writing because hopefully,
having a written memory of that night,
might also help your survival to be a bit easier.

And then I say to my precious wife, Kathy:
"You worked really hard with me and
you encouraged me
when I cried and wanted to quit."

I know just saying "thank you" to all of you
will never be enough.
But I could never have finished
without your support.
I dedicate this book to all of you
who lost loved ones that night, and to those
who actually walked that valley with me.

Reverend R. Douglas Veer
Husband, Father, Friend

# CHAPTER ONE
## WHERE CHARACTER
## IS DEVELOPED WITH INTELLECT

Photo: The Dessert Engineer

  It was beautiful.  That was my first thought as I entered the campus of Toccoa Falls Bible College.

  The large, white stone wall set at a forty-five-degree angle to the road caught my attention. It was on the right side of a well-manicured entrance, and it curved inward, standing about sixteen feet tall.

  I guessed it to be about sixty feet in length. It was impressive, yet not imposing. As we drove onto the campus, there was an air of peace and tranquility. There was even a sense of coming home.

1

## FAMILY COMES FIRST

Toccoa Falls Bible College was the furthest thing from my mind six months earlier, as I climbed structural metal columns, walking, and working, on steel I-beams a few hundred feet in the air.

I was a widower with three children, living in Pell City, Alabama, when I met and married the girl next door. Before long we moved to Cahaba Heights, Alabama, where her father lived, and from there to Talladega, Alabama, where I began building houses for a living. We settled into married life quite nicely; time was treating us well.

In just a short while, we bought our own home with a garden out back, a car, a pick-up truck, and a motorcycle. Within a year we had a precious little girl we named Jaimée Suzanne.

Photo: Veer Family Member

When she would see a picture of Jesus she would call out the name "Zeezus" while reaching toward it to touch his beard. Maybe that was because I had a beard too, but I think there was more to it than that.

She became the heart-lifting delight of our whole family. On the surface, we seemed to have things as good as anyone could ask for.

Before long, I went to work for the Daniel Construction Company, about twenty miles from home, helping to build a multi-million dollar addition onto Kimberly-Clark paper mill, in Childersburg, Alabama. After the first four hours on the job, I was called to the office of Jim Sherwood, who was the Project Manager. Mr. Sherwood offered me the job as Foreman of the crew along with a nice raise in pay. I accepted it.

Our job was to build and install wooden forms to hold concrete. We would lace thick, iron, reinforcement rods together--some of them half the size of a man's wrist. When they were completed, concrete was poured over them into the forms, making thick slabs for the foundations of the buildings. Sometimes those foundations were as much as five feet thick.

Behind us came the ironworkers setting steel columns for the buildings which would eventually stand on the slabs. As the steel rose, we continued forming and pouring, floor after floor of suspended slabs. The buildings rose as much as 200 to 300 feet in the air.

Architects, engineers, building inspectors, designers, and high-rise builders in general, come to the United States from all over the world. They come to learn how to erect buildings of this height, and how to do it so they can sustain the effects of earthquakes. We were one of the sites they came to.

## ROCK-SOLID

The construction of any large building begins with tall machines called pile-drivers. They lift long "H" shaped pilings, or "O" shaped pipes, and stand them on end. Then a single cylinder diesel engine at the top of that machine lifts a huge steel block known as the "hammer", and drops it onto the end of the upright piling, driving the long steel deep into the ground.

At first, one hit from that huge hammer might drive the other end of a piling four or five feet into the ground, depending on the height the hammer was dropped from, and how hard the ground is. But the hammering continues, blow after blow, stopping only for workers to weld together piling after piling, end to end, until the steel is driven farther and farther through soil and rock, deep within the earth. As it goes 40 feet, 50 feet, 100 feet, and 200 feet, the process continues until the hammer strikes three times in succession, driving it down only one inch or less. At that point, the piling hits solid bedrock. Only then, are the conditions considered stable enough to build upon so as to withstand the future rigors of earthquakes.

## WHAT'S THAT NOISE?

As I started writing this book, Kathy, my wife, leaned over my shoulder reading. She was interested in this portion, about the pilings being driven by a machine, and the noise it makes. She said to me, "When I was a young girl growing up in Edmonton, Canada, I used to hear the methodical bang, bang, bang as you just described, and I always wondered what that noise was. Back in the 1980s when I lived there, the population of Edmonton was less than 500,000 people. I guess construction never stopped though because today Edmonton has over one million people. So, I guess I finally have my answer. The bang, bang, bang sound was a pile-driver. How interesting!"

I told her, "Yeah. I loved my work back then because it made me feel like I was part of something very special. No one in the world constructed large, high-rise buildings better than the companies right here in the United States. That's why engineers would come from all over the world to learn from us. And I want you to know this: the Daniels Construction Company of Greenville, South Carolina, has the reputation of being one of the very best builders in the entire world."

She said, "But, it seems like a death-defying job working around that kind of thing, and working up so high."

I said, "Sure it is because everything in life is. It begins the moment you're born. You can't chase it away. You can't run away from it, no matter where you go, so why waste your energy trying? Whether you're working within the steel skeleton of a high rise, 200 feet in the air, or sitting on a yacht in the Atlantic ocean, deep-sea fishing, death is always there; always waiting; just one heartbeat away.


## THE BUILDING CAN MOVE

I explained another interesting fact to her. If you were standing at the top edge of a tall building, the cars and trucks on the ground below would appear to be the size of a fly or an ant. From that position, 200 or 300 feet up, near the edge, you would see that the building was built to be flexible so it could sway back and forth.

For example, if you were looking down the outside wall of the building as it swayed toward you, it would be as if you were looking down a slide, all the way to the ground below. That entire side of the building would be in your view. Then, as the building would sway the opposite direction, out and away from you, it was as if you were suspended in mid-air because you couldn't see the side of the building at all.

Could you fall? Of course! Anything can happen at any time, anywhere. Sure, working under these conditions could have very easily been my walk through a valley of death, and for a couple of men on that job-site, it was. Death is always near, because no matter who you are, or where you are, we're always just one breath away from dying. Dying is part of living.

Sometimes we could see storms in the distant sky while dark clouds passed below us, and occasionally, we could see lightning in them. I've been asked many times if I was afraid of falling. I said, "Number one if I were afraid of falling I wouldn't have been there. Or at least, I shouldn't have been there! But if I were to be welded to the columns with a chain, and God wanted me to fall, I would fall. If He didn't want me to fall, then nothing could shake the building hard enough to bring me down."

That could have been my "macho-man" talking, or perhaps just my youthful ignorance, but I always felt as if God was protecting me while I worked.


## HANGING ON THE EDGE

Our standard work week was ten hours a day from Monday through Thursday which gave us our forty-hour work week with a three day weekend. Everyone on the crew seemed to be happy with the hours, and the work we were accomplishing. That is, they all seemed happy except one young man who worked for me, whose name escapes me, but I'll call him Johnny.

Johnny was a very good worker, always on time, hard working, and well liked. We had just poured a foundation deep into the ground, and the ironworkers had installed the columns and second-floor beams, which were twelve or fourteen feet above the ground slab.

As we began installing forms for the second-floor slab, Johnny began saying that he may be leaving soon, and often gave me different reasons. As the second-floor was about to be poured, Johnny came to me again and said, "Doug, I think this pay-day--Thursday--will be my last day." I asked him why, but just as before, he didn't seem to have a very concrete reason. He just said he felt his time was done there. As we talked, I began to better understand his reason for leaving.

I finally said, "Johnny, you're afraid of heights aren't you?" He said, "Well, I haven't used my G. I. bill for anything yet, and I have been considering going to school. Besides, my wife and I have been talking it over, and she might be finding a job, so we'll make it alright."

I stood there staring at him and again I said, "Johnny, it's the height that bothers you isn't it?" He finally said that it was, and he wasn't going to push his luck. I said; "Okay, Johnny, but I want you to know that I think you're a good worker, and you're making really good money, and everyone here likes you. How about if I make you a deal? I won't reveal your problem with height to anyone, but I'll keep you working in areas where you'll never have to be near the edge where you might look down. Then would you stay? At least as long as you can? I really hate to lose you, Johnny."

Johnny agreed he would try it, and I kept him working only in places that were covered with plywood, wide enough to feel as if he were not even above the ground. Little by little, he would work nearer and nearer to the edge, and by the time we were about four or five stories in the air, which would be about sixty or seventy feet, Johnny was hanging off the side working in a harness and having a good time of it. I've always appreciated the courage he had to persevere and beat his own fears by trusting me. I cared a lot for the men in my crew and would have done anything for them.

## DEATH IN A BUCKET

During my time as Foreman, there was never a man on my crew who was seriously injured until I left and moved to Toccoa, Georgia. Within a couple of weeks, two of them were killed when a careless crane operator "two-blocked" a man-bucket they were being lifted in, and it fell nearly a hundred feet to the ground, killing both of them.

It was reported to me that Bill, who was from my crew, had a pack of welding rods hanging on his hip and they were all driven through him, coming out in the area of his neck, shoulders, and back. When the bucket slammed into the ground the other man's head was broken open, causing instant death. Bill lived long enough to get to the hospital where he also died. I don't know what ever happened to the crane operator as far as charges were concerned.

On large construction jobs, using a crane to hoist workers in a man-bucket is common practice to get workers to high places and it eliminates the need to physically climb. Today, certain safety gear is required to be in place at the end of the boom to prevent what is called "two-blocking".

"Two-blocking" is defined as, "the condition in which the lower load block (or hook) comes in contact with the upper load block (or boom point), interfering with safe operation of the crane load." When two-blocking occurs, force is applied to the hoist, or the hook arrangement, either breaking the hoist line or disengaging the load straps from the hook. This causes the hook to be pulled up and out of place, losing the load, which then falls to the ground below. This can cause serious injury to those who are working in the bucket, or to those standing directly below. If the bucket is high enough, it can even cause death. That's what happened to my crew members Bill, and his work-mate.


## DEATH BY CIGARETTE

Yes, the valley of death is always present; always waiting for us. We just don't ever know it in the moment. Through the years I haven't tried hard enough to stay in contact with the men in my crew, but I wish I had. I recently made contact with Joe Teel, who still lives in that same area of Alabama. He told me, Rick Riggins, another crewman still lives near him. I remember Rick well. Thinking back, it was Rick who helped me quit smoking . . . well, in a way he did.

I was walking a four inch wide I-beam, probably eighty or ninety feet in the air, trying to light a cigarette with a book matches. The wind, of course, was blowing out every match I lighted when suddenly my foot missed the I-beam, and I stood there tottering on one foot. I looked down. Then I looked at the cigarette. Then I looked up, and I said, "God, one way or another, these things are going to kill me. I guess that's what you're trying to tell me."

I made my way back to the "gang-box" where we kept out tools and personal effects during the day and got my extra pack of cigarettes, my other matches, and my lighter. I gave them all to Rick because he smoked the same brand I did. That's where and when I quit smoking. So, "Thanks, Rick. Even though it was a terrible gift to shove your way--giving you my smokes--it did help me quit. I hope you have also quit by now."

There are other crewmen I think of often: some who left the job, some who completed it, and some who died there. You know for every large job that has two or three thousand workers, there will always be three or four deaths. Yes, it all brings back memories and I'll always remember my fellow-workers and my friends.

## PAINTING AND PRETENDING

A couple of years passed and the Daniels' job was coming to an end, so I began planning ahead. The well-known phrase, "time and tide wait for no man," applied to me as well, so without wasting time, I began to look at where I wanted my life to go next.

Years before, I had done some undercover work as an informant. I investigated and turned in drug dealers selling street narcotics. I decided to get back into this kind of work but it didn't go over well with my wife. She was afraid of what could happen to me when I went out at night trying to make buys from dealers.

I know it sounds terrible, but I was a user myself at one time. Because of that, I knew how damaging drugs could be so I thought I could be of help by trying to put an end to drugs and the harm they were causing our kids. To me, my past experience was one of the best tools I had, to get the necessary information I needed to arrest the dealers.

At the same time, I was doing custom painting on vans, motorcycles, and dune buggies. The "trick painting" as it was called, was done working with an airbrush, which is a small pen-sized, pen-shaped paint gun. With it, very fine, intricate design work could be done; even portrait painting. It's an interesting tool, and it was very interesting to use. Several years before, I had attended Dallas Art
Institute, because I've always had a natural artistic flair. So part of my "cover" as a Narc was being a "trick painter".

With pictures of various custom paintings in my pocket, I was ready to go. Now all that was left was to do a good job of pretending I was a user, and convince them that I also had drugs to sell. Convincing the dealer I needed that steady source of drugs to pay for my own addiction would hopefully get me into places where the suppliers were. The
painting was easy, but I wasn't too sure how the pretending would go.

I enjoyed both careers: the custom paint work, and the extra money to go with it, and the undercover work because I was able to put a stop some of the beatings and murders that went along with drug life. Could I change the whole world? No, but maybe I could at least help a few. My home life suffered, though. Because of the kind of people I was spending time with each week, my wife was very unhappy.

## BLOWN AWAY

One night in Talladega, Alabama, a meeting was arranged with a supplier from Atlanta. My young partner and I had been there thirty minutes or so and he was becoming intoxicated letting his mouth say more than he should be saying. It's called "blowing your cover." Within another fifteen minutes, two more men came to the house and I knew by their attitude that we were in trouble. By their appearance, they were what we would call, "possible Chicago dudes". When the main man introduced us, I put my hand out to the guy closest to me to shake hands with him.

"Hey, dude. I'm Jimmy what's happening?" He took my hand and in an instant, my arm was twisted behind my back! "Hey man let go! What's the problem?" I asked.

As he released my arm he said, "I just wanted to look at your hand man. Wanted to see if you had a workin' man's hand or not. You're cool."

With that, he patted me on the cheek as a way of apology, but a fist full of my beard stayed in his hand as he pulled my head down to about his chest level.

"Owww! Man, what *is* your problem?!" I said.

Again he replied, "Awe, nothin' meant by it bro'. Just checkin' you out."

By then I knew something was up and the dealer had probably become suspicious of us. I continued talking while I worked my way nearer to the door and at the right time I bolted! Running off the porch into the bare dirt yard, I went up over a car, running as fast as I could while they began shooting at me. I had the awful feeling that at any minute I'd feel a bullet in my back, but it didn't happen. I've always said that God protects fools and little children and I guess that particular night I was very foolish operating with a young boy who was getting high and drunk while we were working. He may have blown our cover, but I could have also been blown away in the process. Was I scared? You bet I was.

## FOR THE LOVE OF MONEY

Before I got home I began to think about a past experience I had on another drug-buying night. It was painful just remembering it and I began questioning if I should be doing this kind of work.

A late summer evening took me into a crack house. I was hoping to meet with someone who was supposed to be a supplier, but the house was empty as I walked through the filth ridden place. I found no one there, except one small body that had died.

The little body probably didn't weigh over 50 pounds and was black and blue from drugs and physical abuse. I sat there and cried. I cried for the loss of this precious child--this unknown someone who was loved and would be missed. I cried for the parents, who, in their grief would suffer for years and years to come. I cried for myself because I was so helpless to prevent things like this from happening.

I reached out to touch the little foot. I guess I was hoping to find some life in it, but it was cold. I held this lifeless foot in my hand, which at one time had run across grassy yards playing with other children, or had run across a room, wrapping its arms around Momma's waist, asking for a piece of candy or the brushing of hair.

Now, there was no one but me to try to understand the last few painful steps of this young one, who walked deep into the valley of death, here in a place where men loved money more than the life of a child.

## IS HELL DEEP ENOUGH

A pain I can't describe in words bit deep into my heart and emotions. I cried out loud to God, "Why? Why do these kinds of deaths have to happen? I'm out here trying to do this great, public, humanitarian thing, and I'm failing miserably? That's right. Failing! I must be, because this is still happening? Why God!? I just don't understand . . . am I crazy? I know the course of death winds its way around to everyone, and takes its toll. It is no respecter of persons. But why *this* one? What can I do to reach them before this happens? Please . . ."

My words echoed back at me, bouncing off of the tile walls in the emptiness of that filthy bathroom. I sat there still holding that colorless foot, pitifully lost in my sorrow.

My tears landed on the dirty floor making dark, damp circles. I said, "God, how are you going to decide where this little one will go? Surely you will show your, kindness and understanding when this child comes before you! Surely you won't withhold your mercy . . . after the hell on earth this one has already been through!

"And what about the men who lured her into this dying place? What about them? Do you have a hell painful enough, long enough, and hot enough for them? Do you have a hell deep enough to punish them for what they've done to this little life?"

For all my anguished questions, only the silence of the soiled room responded.  I was at a complete loss. So I wept.

After a time I realized I needed to find a telephone so I could call for someone to come and deal with this. As I walked away, I was leaving the child behind, but I knew the memory of that event would never leave my mind as long as I lived.

I was reminded of a poem written by someone who must have had an experience with the death of a child, and must have had the compassion to able to spell out my feelings in so few words. To the best of my memory it went something like this:

A simple child
that lightly draws its breath,
and feels its life in every limb;
what should it know of death?

"Now run above, my little maid.
Your limbs, they are alive;
but when you are in the church-yard laid,
I'll surely sit and cry."

## MY WIFE WAS RIGHT

That night--even remembering my past experiences--I still didn't think too much about why my wife felt the way she did, so I brushed the thought aside. I felt someone had to step up and do something to help put an end to the devastation caused by drugs in the lives of so many. I thought I should at least help stop some of it where and when I could. And the adrenalin rush I got from seeing such people get put out of business and into a prison cell was at least as good or better than the rush from doing those same drugs myself. I loved what I was doing, yet at times it did bother me.

I walked away from the crime scene, and began to explore the deeper recesses of my mind; that place where no one else gets to go. I felt the fresh night air on my face. My mind turned to thoughts of family, life, and my real responsibilities. I thought, "Maybe my wife is right. Maybe there's too much danger here for my family. Maybe I need to get out of this business."

News travels faster on the street than it does in the newspapers. My wife had already heard about what had happened before I got home. Again she explained how afraid she was, and how what happened the night before could have meant I wouldn't come home. I knew she was right. Yes, I got away safely but I realized the valley of death is always ready to take a person if they're ready to walk in it. I was not ready for that yet.

It was time for me to put away the rough and tumble bearded, long-haired, undercover cop image and begin to think like a husband and father. It was time to let someone else to do that job. It was time for me to agree with my wife that the family might be in harm's way because of the people I was associating with. So I quit.

I continued to feel burdened though. I thought someone must know how to help people find a better way of living rather than using drugs. People need a better way to deal with their problems instead of hiding behind an addiction. I knew there was a way and I wanted to know what it was.

# CHAPTER TWO
## DON'T LOOK BACK

It may have been mid-May or June--shortly after my decision to quit doing this kind of work--that four young men came from Toccoa Falls College to sing at our church in Talladega; they spent the night with us. Steve Reibsome, Steve Withrow, Mike Davis and Butch Taylor were terrific young gentlemen with a youthful fire and joy just beaming out of them. It was a pleasure to know and spend time with them.

These men had been such a positive influence that my wife and I talked about actually going to Bible college ourselves, and I became drawn to the idea, though I was nearly forty years old and married with four children.

Please let me assure you, I wasn't wanting to go there with the idea of becoming a great, well-known preacher. Not at all. I didn't have thoughts of seeing my name and title of Pastor on a marquee. Nor did I think I was going to set the world on fire with eloquence and wisdom that would pour forth from my lips. No. But in my heart, I thought this could be a chance to change part of the world which was my strength to go on.

I knew in my heart this would be a life-changing decision for me. If I decided to move away from Talladega, I would have to leave and never look back. As I thought about it, I was reminded of some words of wisdom by Henry Wadsworth:

Look not mournfully into the past;
it comes not back again,
but to wisely improve the future is thine.
Go forth to improve the shadowy future,
without fear, and with a manly heart.

## A NEW ADVENTURE

My hope was to see people's lives changed; to reach those who had lost their way and needed someone to point them in a better direction. I wanted to be there for them before I found any other victims, like that cold, expired body--the only visible proof that life had ever been there in the first place. All hope for a better life was taken from *that* little one.

I wanted to reach young people in general, and rescue them from crack houses or from an alley somewhere. I wanted to reach those who were the victims of a death-by-drugs lifestyle. And I knew that less than five percent of those who were addicted to drugs were actually receiving any professional help.

I wanted to find them before their lives were ruined by those who could care less about them. I knew I couldn't change the past, but I was hoping I could help change the future, at least for a few.

The real answer, though, is a spiritual one. Some of you may not agree, but the only sure-fire way I know of to completely break away from any destructive habit is to give one's life over to Jesus Christ. But please realize this: it has to be a complete surrender of one's own will, letting God have control instead of the drugs. There's no strength to save you by going it alone when it comes to facing your own *valley of drug-death*.

I also thought about the many older dealers who have already lived out their years and are nearing their final days. Many live day by day, hour by hour, feeling as if there is no hope ahead, having no idea where they will go when they draw their last breath. I don't mean just lying in a box on the cold hard ground under a cover of unfeeling, uncaring green sod. It's that many don't know where they will go beyond that.

Yes, what happens beyond the grave? What then? What about the great ever-after, where God waits to talk with us about what we've done with our lives?

I already had a young wife buried in Beloit, Wisconsin and a daughter buried in Dallas Texas. I knew where my daughter was, but what of my young wife? Where did she go after her last breath? I honestly don't know.

So why did I care about the drug dealers? I was surprised at my own heart of concern. But I actually wanted to reach out to the ones supplying drugs and causing destruction to innocent victims. I guess you could say "Go figure," but I cared.

Yeah, so I guess my wife was right. Life at the moment was getting far too complicated and had become more than she had bargained for. It was time for a change. Maybe college life would bring better things. So before long we were selling our house in Talladega, Alabama, and renting a U-haul truck, bound for a new adventure in Toccoa, Georgia. And what an adventure it would be.


## OOPS! FORGOT THAT

I now had many years of experience in construction, so a simple telephone interview before leaving Talladega was enough to win me the position of Director of the Physical Plant at Toccoa Falls College. This is just a fancy way of saying I was in charge of maintenance for the campus and the surrounding 1,100 acres.

I met with the College President, Dr. Opperman, who told me I would be expected to shave my beard and cut my hair which at the time was in a pony-tail. I had a full beard and long hair which I had worn for quite a few years, ever since my Hippie days. It was hard for me to agree to that, but if I was to take the job I had to do it on their terms. I agreed and shook hands with him. It was settled.

Then I met with the director of financial affairs, who would be my direct supervisor. He had someone give me a tour of the campus. I was informed of everything I would be responsible for, including the administration building, all of the school buildings, the gymnasium, the dormitories, the cafeteria, other student housing areas, individual family homes, and the mobile home park where many married students lived.

In addition to the 1,100 acres of college property I would oversee all the electrical work, plumbing, painting, carpentry, and even ditch digging, when it became necessary; it would all fall on my desk to be dealt with. My responsibility was to keep the college running properly. It was a lot to consider but I gladly accepted the job.

There was one item, though, that I was never informed of. There was an old dirt road leading to a dam, high above the campus, holding back a 440-acre lake which fed the Toccoa Falls waterfall, for which both the city and the College were named. Although the dam was an impressive four hundred feet long, forty feet high, and twenty feet thick, I was never taken there, nor told of its existence. How could they have missed telling me about that?

## TA-QUA-HI

Many years before any of us were here, the Cherokee Indians found the waterfall and named it "Ta-Qua-Hi" which I have always heard said, that in their language meant "beautiful". The true meaning of some of the old Cherokee names were long since lost by the time the white people came.

There are three places named Toccoa. The Toccoa River, the Toccoa waterfall, and the City of Toccoa. These are all in the same area and were all named by the Cherokee Indians. There's no doubt these are beautiful places, but the Cherokee word from which the name is taken, does not mean "beautiful". The Cherokee word for "beautiful" is "u-wo-duhi."

Among the Cherokee, their longest lasting enemies were the Catawba Indians and the word the Cherokee spoke for Catawba was "A-ta-qua," which was often shortened to "Ta-qua." Often, the Catawba war parties invaded the Cherokee territory, sometimes even trying to set up a village and live there. The Cherokee did not take kindly to the Catawba trying to take their land and they often wiped the invaders out completely.

The place where the Catawbas tried to come in was called "Catawba place," or "place of the Catawba". In Cherokee, it was "Ta-qua-hi". When spoken by the Cherokee the syllables were drawn out and spoken as Ta-qu-a. To the whites, Ta-qua-a, "the place of the Catawba," sounded like, "Ta-co-a", which is nothing like the word "u-wo-duhi." With this misunderstanding of the Cherokee, the name Ta-qu-a, became Toccoa, which white men took for granted meant beautiful. Then in 1738, the Cherokee sold the land with the Ta-qu-a river, and the Ta-qu-a waterfall, to early American settlers, which in time became part of Georgia.

## A CREEK RUNS BEHIND US

After being hired, we rented a house on campus, owned by Dr. Kerr, just a few hundred yards from the maintenance building where my office was. Directly behind my house, actually in my back yard about thirty feet from my house, a bubbling little creek twenty feet wide wound its way downstream making the setting more enjoyable than I can explain. As I said before, I felt as though we were living in a little piece of heaven right here on earth. But that same peaceful creek which sang us to sleep each night would eventually run angry red with the blood of death.

It was mid-July, 1977, and the new school year would be starting in a couple of weeks. My oldest son, nearly eighteen, was out of school. My fourteen-year-old daughter was in eighth grade. Kirk, my youngest son was ten years old and a fifth grader; and on February 13, just seven months away, my youngest daughter Jaimée would have her second birthday. She was supposed to be born Saturday, February 14, 1976, but a motorcycle ride the day before caused us to go to the hospital and receive her a day early. Never-the-less, I always thought of her as my Valentine Angel.

It seemed as though all was well with us here in our little piece of paradise. The routine of my job was going smoothly and all seemed to be going well on campus. There were work trucks to keep repaired, leaky pipes to mend, paint to be touched up, and other normal maintenance work to be done which kept me satisfied with the responsibilities of my new job. All the men working under me were dependable and skilled at their job, making it easier for me to do mine.

Our home was a very comfortable three bedroom brick house with a nice yard, small bushes and trees all around. Added to that, we put in flowering plants along the front porch and sidewalk, putting our own little touch to what was already a very attractive environment to be living in. The driveway coming from the street ended in a wide attached carport with plenty of room for my pastime: playing with motorcycles and working on various carpentry projects.

Bill and Peggy Ehrensberger and their four kids lived right across the creek in a big old house with wood siding. It was probably built eighty or ninety years before. Bill was a student and one of my plumbers and he and I quickly bonded in a friendship that deepened as we spent time together.

## SOMETHING EXCITING TO TELL!

I think Bill and Peggy were from St. Mary's, either in Pennsylvania or Ohio. They were still living there when one evening, Bill was on his way home from work and was listening to Billy Graham on the car radio. He became so interested that he pulled onto the shoulder of the road to pay full attention. Bill said that during that broadcast, he accepted Jesus as his Savior and was anxious to get home and tell Peggy about it.

When he got home, Peggy, in an especially excited mood, met him at the door, wanting to tell him some good news of her own. What was the news? She had just become saved too! When they compared their stories, it turns out Peggy was at home listening to the very same Billy Graham program Bill had listened to on the car radio, and both of their lives changed at the same time, so they decided to eventually come to Toccoa Falls College to study.

At some point before they actually moved onto the college property, Bill and Peggy supervised a children's home, just outside of Toccoa, and were receiving hardly any money for their efforts. There were many times when the food given to them to cook had already begun to spoil, but somehow they managed to make do with what was brought to them.

A man named Mr. Nickles, whom I tagged as "Mister Penny-pincher" was either the overseer or perhaps the owner of the children's home. He rarely came up with funds for them. It was nearly a starvation situation, but Bill and Peggy kept plugging along until the home was finally closed by the authorities. That's when Bill came on board the maintenance crew at Toccoa Falls College as a plumber.

And that's just one story of one family, but many other lives were pulled together from all over the country, even as far away as Thailand, in Asia, and Chad, in central Africa. And they were all there the weekend of November 6, 1977, on that particular campus, at that particular time. Each person was going to have a very necessary part to play in the events which would unfold during that tragic time. I'm fully convinced God made no mistake in having each of us present.


## REALLY GOOD EATIN'

On Friday, November 4, the rain had let up for a couple of hours and I was playing in the creek behind my house with Jaimée, my two-year-old daughter. I piled rocks across the creek, just near the little road-bridge that passed over it, fashioning a dam which brought the water level higher and broadened the banks of the creek just enough to make a safe place for her to play. For an hour or more we played in the creek creating many precious memories which will be with me forever, just as if it were yesterday.

Later that same day, I was looking into the creek between Bill and Peggy's house and mine, when I spotted a big turtle nearly as big around as a wash-tub. I managed to get it to bite down on a long wooden pole and pulled it ashore. I spent the next hour or so cleaning it and getting it ready to cook. I don't know if you've ever eaten things such as frog legs, gator tail, or turtle, but in some parts of the country, they're considered a delicacy. In Georgia, we just call them "really good eatin'."

Before long I had a big pot cooking on the stove, and I asked Bill if they would like to come over for supper and maybe bring something to go with turtle stew. That's when I discovered they were really struggling financially so I offered to cook the whole meal. What else could I do? I cooked vegetables, made biscuits and desert, and invited them to have supper with us. But since their house was larger, and set up to feed more people, we took all the food over there. And the feast was on!

Peggy taught me something about receiving which I'll never forget. Most people are good at giving but many are very poor and uncomfortable in receiving, especially if they know, that you know, they are needy. Not so with Peggy! She squealed with delight when they were invited to supper, and profusely thanked us in a true manner of happiness.

I had never experienced that before! It taught me that there is truly a gift of showing appreciation when you receive something. Seeing the excitement coming from Peggy, as open, and real and innocent as that of a little child, I knew I'd have to learn how to relax and be like that too. I think it's a gift most people don't have, but I wanted it.

During supper, they talked about the fireplace in their house which had apparently been closed many years before. They wondered if it could be opened for use again, because of winter coming on. Bill asked if I would help him reopen the roof where the chimney had been covered over, and remove whatever was covering the fireplace so they could start using wood for heat. We all agreed it would be done. And as the evening ended, all the leftovers from supper were left for them.


**THE FIREPLACE**

The next day, Saturday, November 5, we all went to work. First, the fireplace was opened. Then Bill and I went up on the roof to uncover the brick chimney so we could extend it above the roof-line and make it a functioning fireplace once again.

While we were working, a chunk of old chimney brick fell down and black soot went all through the house, even getting inside the kitchen cabinets and under the sink. It was a mess!  Bill and Liz Anderson and others living on campus came to help Peggy clean the house. It wound up being a neighborhood experience, which is no surprise because the students and staff living there were like one big family. If one was in plenty, all were in plenty, and if one had a problem we all pitched in until it was solved. The fireplace was made to work again and now they could have heat from it all winter.

While we were all cleaning Bill and Peggy's house, I washed out the kitchen cupboards and it was then I discovered that all the food they had was one can of green beans. I don't know how far that would have gone for a meal the evening before, but the turtle stew certainly did the job.

My wife and I had been to a railroad salvage store that week and bought several cases of canned food. We also had a freezer full of beef roasts, chicken, and other meats, so we divided everything in half, canned goods, beef, chicken, vegetables and all, and took it to Bill and Peggy. Again, there was the unhindered squeal of delight from Peggy. I can hear it even now these many years later. I guess I'll never forget it; at least I hope not. Now, Bill, Peggy, Robby, Kirstin, Kenny, and Tommy had a cupboard full of food and the squeal made it all worthwhile.

Before we left that evening, there was a time of worship, and prayer, and giving thanks to God for supplying our needs. We also gave thanks for having a true friendship, which is very seldom found in the world today. A friendship such as we had is when you all are of the same mind and can express your deepest inner self to one another, including your spiritual self.

C.S. Lewis was a Christian writer and speaker. He died on November 22, 1963, the same day President John F. Kennedy was killed. He wrote this about worshiping God:

"A man can no more diminish God's glory
by refusing to worship Him
than a lunatic can put out the sun
by scribbling the word 'darkness'
on the walls of his cell."

Bill and Peggy wrote in strong letters of brightness, the love they had for God, and it was my joy and privilege to have been counted as their friend.


## LITTLE RED RIDING HORSE
After Bill and Peggy's house was clean we went home and had supper. When that was done my wife

and I went into town to buy school supplies for our kids. The last place we went was the J. C. Penny store, for new school clothing.

While we were there, Jaimée, our two-year-old daughter, found and climbed onto a little red plastic riding horse with yellow wheels, and claimed it as her own. I hope you know that any two-year-old rules the roost when they want to, and that's exactly what she wanted!

She sat on it, wrapped her little legs around it, and would not let go! She refused to get off. There was no choice but to lift her, riding horse and all, up onto the counter and pay for it; we had to lift her little bottom up to see the price tag.

We bought the riding horse for her, plus school clothes for the other kids, and everything else they needed. Our night of shopping was done, and it was time to go home and reminisce about all that had happened that day. What a great day it had been in our own little "Garden of Eden".


## EXPLOSIONS IN THE SKY

On our way home I had the wipers on full but they still weren't keeping the windshield clear enough to see the road. As we came to the top of the hill heading down to the campus, I pulled off on the shoulder of the road, across from the cemetery and parked. I felt it was a little too dangerous to drive in the blinding rain which was so heavy that it prevented us from even making out the shapes of other cars. Their headlights were just blinding glimmers on our windshield.

As we sat there we saw flashes of light in the sky over the campus that didn't seem to be lightning. I later learned they were Georgia Power transformers, carrying electrical power to the college, including our home, and they were exploding where they sat at the top of the telephone poles.

We could see that all the power had gone out in that part of town, so we sat for about twenty minutes. Finally, seeing we were accomplishing nothing, sitting there in the rain, I decided to drive slowly down the hill to the campus and home.

We got home safely in spite of the exploding transformers and the torrents of rain beating on our car, but it was pitch-dark. There were no street lights, no house lights anywhere, and it was blacker than anything I had seen in a long time. It had been raining like this for ten days and nights, and everyone was ready for it to stop.

Pulling into our driveway I left the car lights on so we could see how to get into the house. Because of having no electricity in the house, once inside, I lighted candles in several rooms. Even without power, it was so good to be home, safe, and out of the storm.

Of course, the little riding horse had to be ridden for awhile before bedtime and Jaimée had a lot of fun with it. The truth is we had fun, too, just watching her enjoy her new toy. But then before we knew It, it was time for bed.

Being careful to avoid any tragedy I went through all the rooms putting out the candles except for one in the hallway. There in the hall, I placed a small end-table with a fat candle on it so we would have light during the night to see our way to the bathroom. The rain and wind continued but we settled in, thinking tomorrow would be a much better day.

Jaimée was a breastfed baby and slept in bed with us most nights so she snuggled down between us. But tonight it was a little harder on the other children as they settled into their beds because they were not too happy with the eerie darkness in their rooms. It was sort of like the Christmas story where Mom and Dad had just settled down for a long winter's nap.

I've always been a sound sleeper and my sleep has always been especially peaceful with the rain beating on the roof. But tonight was different. I didn't have the peace I generally enjoyed. The rain seemed to be pounding harder as if it was trying to get in, and the wind seemed to be more ferocious as it whipped through the trees just outside our bedroom window. But I was tired and it was late, so sleep began to have its way, dulling my senses to the unusual weather happening outside. The house was warm and comforting; all seemed well here in our little piece of paradise. We didn't know it, but this nap wasn't going to last very long.

# CHAPTER THREE
## TWO WORLDS COLLIDE

About 1:30 in the morning the entire household was awakened by what sounded like two worlds colliding and I guess they were. It was the world of normalcy, and the world of total chaos, clashing with one another. At first, I thought I was dreaming. Then I clearly heard my children yelling out, "Dad! Dad!! It's a tornado!"

My gut tightened and I got out of bed and turned to the bedroom window. There in the spooky darkness was an even stranger looking "train", silhouetted against the dark sky, passing through the campus from left to right. I started feeling sick inside, as I stared at the rough looking engine followed by a long string of passenger cars. Even though I wasn't at ease with it, I wanted to calm the kids down so I said, "Go back to sleep kids; it's only the train going past."

Still half asleep, turning my back to the window, I started to get back into bed. With one knee on the bed and a foot still on the floor, I felt very unsettled over what I saw. I went back to the window again to have another look. Fear gripped me as I looked out at the long, dark object, silhouetted against the ominous looking sky, half lighted by the glow of lights from town. I suddenly realized the awful truth: "There's no train on campus! And whatever that thing is, it's coming sideways at us!"

I tried to focus into the darkness to see what this thing was when suddenly I felt water under my feet. In no time at all the water was up to the calf of my legs. I knew I had to do something immediately or we would have a house full of water! But what? How could I stop it?

My mind began spinning with thoughts of what I needed to do to protect my family. By then the water was already nearly to my waist. "It's all my fault!" I thought. "The little dam I built across the creek for Jaimée and I to play in must have overflowed! And now it was coming into the house! Why did I put so many of the big rocks in it? Why did I leave it there? I'll have to break it apart tomorrow. But Geez, look what I've caused now!"

## I CAN'T GET TO THEM ALL!

The house was pitch dark. There wasn't even any light from the outside coming through, to help me see. I needed to move as much as possible up above the water, but first, the kids had to be safe. Then I thought the safest place to get everyone out would be through the attic.

I thought, "The end table in the hall has the candle on it. That's it! If I stand on that I can pull down the attic stairs and get everyone up there. It's so dark! Where's the table? My God, it's gone! I have to have it because there's no rope on the pull-down stairs to the attic!"

Then I found the table, or actually, it found me, as it floated down the hall and bumped into me. I pulled the end-table over to where I knew the attic stairway should be and got it set into place, holding it down while I stepped up onto it, thinking, "I hope it holds me up without breaking. I have to find the cracks where the door fits the ceiling so I can pull the stairs down because the rope is gone."

The ceiling was rough with its blown on texture of small rocks. It began to tear at my fingers. "Ouch! My fingernails are breaking! No! I can't quit! I can't! I

32

have to find the ladder! OK! It's opening. Now to get everyone into the attic so they don't get wet. Hurry! Hurry!!"

I already had my wife and daughter, Jaimée, beside me so I pushed them up the stairs and into the darkness of the hole above my head. Suddenly the water was up to my neck and I was lost in it!  All I could hear now above the roar of the water was, "Dad! Dad! Oh my God, Dad, help me!!"  cried my seventeen-year-old son. I couldn't get to him!

By now the water was being forced into our house, and down through the hallway I was standing in. It was powerful! I thought, "Where's Kirk? Where's Anita? I can't get to them all! God? What can I do? Where are my kids? What's going to happen to us?" I felt so helpless . . .


## THE NIGHTMARE IS ALIVE!

The house shook and the windows gave way as a wall of water poured out its angry power on everything in its path. Nothing could stand before the onslaught of the fifty-five-foot wall of water, moving at one hundred-ten miles an hour, as it swept down through the valley, seething, twisting and turning to follow that once peaceful creek-bed.

Trees, boulders, and homes all became tangled, mangled relics of what they once used to be. Nothing could stand before the thousands of pounds of pressure per square foot screaming out of control through what had been my peaceful valley. Cars, trucks, and Greyhound buses all became flotsam in a sea of irate waters rushing to a new destination.

Now the waters were free from the confines of the weakened earthen dam which we all depended on to hold everything back, for far too many years.

Tonight was the night the pressure of the four hundred-forty-acre lake won, and the eighty year-old dam built of Georgia clay lost. This cold, rainy November night would take thirty-nine innocent lives as its victims. The sweet dream was over; the nightmare was here. Tonight, destiny had come for us.

## PUSH HARDER!

Anita, my fourteen-year-old, was the closest. I thought, "If I turn left, I should be right in her room. Thank God! Yes! Here she is." The water was nearly over my head as I reached for her. I thought, "She must be standing on her bed because she's above the water! Now if I can get back to the stairway with her! Here it is. Push! Push! Push! I must push her up in there. She seems so heavy! I always thought things were lighter to lift in the water! I don't know if she can make it up there. I have to keep pushing and trying anyway. God, she seems so heavy! But I have to get her to safety no matter what happens to me! "

(Many days later, Anita told me what really happened that night. While I was pushing so hard and thinking she was so heavy, I was actually crushing her against the top of the framework of her bedroom door opening. I had missed the opening in the ceiling where the pull-down attic stairway was supposed to be.)

All the books lining the hallway came off the shelves, flying at me like a bunch of bats being disturbed from their cavern ceiling. At the same time, the roots of a tree-trunk came through the end wall, sailing directly at me like a guided missile.

Then, it was either the side walls or the ceiling that had been crushed as I went under the water and was swept away. I could feel the massive weight as it lay on top of me pinning me down, and just as suddenly, it was gone. I tried to understand what was happening, but it became a tumultuous confusion, as I twisted one way, then another, controlled by the force of raging waters gone mad. Nothing was real.

My thoughts were running rampant. "Oh my God! The whole world has come loose! What's happening? I can't see! I feel like I'm in a blender! No, that's crazy! But what is happening?"

I must have been swept down the long hallway and into the kitchen/dining area. I felt familiar objects such as the couch cushions, pictures, and kitchen chairs as they banged against me. Everything was swirling and spinning under the force of the water trying to drive its way free from the room. As the seconds passed my mind was working at top speed.

Then a smooth flat surface came to rest against me and I ran my hands over it. I was puzzled. What could it be? It dawned on me as the hard surface flipped back and forth against me under the swirling water.

"Oh God, it's the glass table top from the kitchen! We just bought that! Please don't let it break! And if it does, don't let it cut me! If it's broken, I'm a goner!"

"What direction is up! Where am I? Oh God, what's happening!"

The fear of being trapped in the room under tons of debris began to fill my mind. Then instantly, I was loosed from the house. Caught by the force of the violent water, it was as if I had been shot out of a canon and was set free. Free perhaps, but could I ever get my directions figured out? Tumbling and turning, I had no idea where I was. And there was no way of escape as I was swept away by this horrific force. One thing I did know for sure is that I wanted to be out of this savage, deadly water.

## ALL OF MY FAMILY ARE DEAD

Twenty or thirty feet under the twisting water, my body began to shriek at me for mercy. "Oh God, I need some air. My lungs hurt. I can't hold my breath anymore."

It seemed as though my physical senses and my mental senses had become separated. My body was being battered, torn, cut, and beaten by debris from broken houses and trees. My mind was writhing in pain, trying to make reasonable sense of it all.

"What's going on? Where's all the water coming from? Where am I? Am I in a lake? Am I dreaming?" I didn't know . . . and in the intense darkness, the answers never came . . .

The desire for air was so strong that I started drinking gulps of water just to have something passing down my throat, as breathing should have done. But there was no breath in it so again my mind said, "Oh God it burns! Help me, please. I need air! Has the whole world ended?"

Then, under the bitter black fifty feet of churning water, I felt something scrape against me that I believed was the ground or the concrete of the street. "Had I hit the bottom?" I wondered. But I knew it was all over. I knew it was time to give up.

There was so much pain in my lungs that I couldn't survive any longer without oxygen so I decided to suck in one huge open-mouthed breath, breathing in the life-ending water instead of air. The end of life for me had come and I calmly accepted it. "Open mouth . . . deep breath in . . . take in the water and die . . ." Then I passed out!

## BIG CHAINS

I don't know how long I was unconscious, but I "came to" as I was being driven head first into something that wasn't moving! I was hurting all over again. My head erupted with pain that made me think, "My God, What is that? There's something in the middle of the river that's not moving! Hang on! Hang on! Hang on! Don't let go! It feels like the big chains on a forklift. Yeah right! Here in the middle of the river? No way! Ha, ha, ha! No really, it can't be! But it does; it feels just like it! They're greasy! I can put my fingers in between the links. Yes! It is! It's the forklift from the shop! Climb it! Climb up! Get up! Get up!!"

The top of the forklift was sticking out of the water, just enough for me to breathe again. "Ah! Air! Oh my God, look at this. I'm in the middle of a lake! How can I get out of here? How did I get in here? Where is this lake? Where is all my family? I guess they're all dead. Oh God, how can I get help? What's going to happen to my life when I get out of here? What will I do without my kids?"

In that moment I wasn't even sure if I was a Christian? Well yes, I was saved by the blood of Jesus. But was my life His? Well, yes it was. But in the midst of my doubt, I was surprised at the unexpected words of faith that slipped out of my mouth.

I said, "Jesus . . . I love you. What do you want God? Do you want me to be alone so I'll go onto the mission field? Whatever . . . whatever . . . I guess my whole family is dead, so what does it matter? Why did I ever come here? Perhaps only You know, but here I am. I belong to You, Lord and I'm ready to serve You."

I thought of a Bible passage that states that there is peace to be found in our relationship with God, and it's a peace that passes all understanding. That's exactly where I was. There was a peace that I couldn't make sense of here in these murky waters of destruction. But His peace was real.

## DADDY, I'M COLD!

Floating around me were about two dozen, fifty-five-gallon barrels. Where they came from I had no idea. I thought, "If I can get hold of one of them and ride it like a bucking horse, I can ride it out of here!  But what if I fall off?  I don't want to be out there again!  This is the only place in the world that's not moving. No! I'm not going to let go. I'm going to hang on right here."

Then something else got my attention, and I said to myself, "Listen! Listen! Yeah, it is! It's a voice out there!  That's crazy!  Wait a minute. Listen . . . Yes, it is someone! Someone's crying! My God, it's a little kid! There's something sticking up over there. My God, that must be about fifty yards away. Why did I let those barrels go by? I've got to get over there. Wow, the water is moving fast. Oh, I see some boards! Yeah, If I can get one of them I might make it. But wait! They're not just boards. They're part of a roof! My God, how can it be? Are all the houses ruined? Ok! I have to swim. I'm a good swimmer so I can make it over there to the noise."

It didn't take long and I was at the object sticking out of the water, and talking to myself again I said, "Good! I made it! Listen to that little voice crying and praying." Then in absolute shock, I cried out loud, "Oh my God! It's my son, Kirk!" I cried out to him, "Kirk hang on! I'm coming!"

There inside a big old four-by-four army troop transport is where Kirk had found refuge. He told me something had wrapped around him as he was picked up and swept away. The rushing waters had wrapped him in an American flag that had been pinned to his bedroom wall.

He also remembered feeling with his feet, what seemed to be the bathroom medicine cabinet mirror and he didn't want to kick it or push on it because it might break. Although underwater, he knew he was being funneled out of the bathroom window.

The waters carried him along and then he said he bumped into something. His hand came across what seemed like the handle of our car door, so he pulled it, opened it, and got inside! It was actually the door handle of a big old army truck. Once inside the cab, he found the canvas roof had been torn and had trapped enough of an air bubble there to sustain him until the waters started going down.

I got to the truck and there saw my boy next to the open window. I crawled in through that same window and sat my self down next to him as he moved over. Sure enough, it was my ten-year-old son, Kirk.

He said, "Daddy, I'm cold. I'm so cold." With strength I didn't know I possessed, I tore the canvas roof completely out of the truck and wrapped his shivering body in it.

"Daddy, I was praying for what to do. You said we should give God thanks for everything, so I was thanking Him for the flood, and as soon as I was done I was going to jump back into the water because I just knew that all of you were dead and I didn't want to be alive either if you were all gone."

My son was referring to a Bible study we had just finished from Philippians 4:6-7 which says, "Be careful for nothing; but in every thing by prayer and supplication with thanksgiving let your requests be made known unto God. And the peace of God, which passeth all understanding, shall keep your hearts and minds through Christ Jesus." We had studied about having a peace that passes all understanding. And here he was--such a young person--yet willing to try and do what God's word said.

It was more than my heart could take as the tears began to run down my wet face. I broke for him as I thought, "God, I love this little guy so much. I guess it's just me and him now. I don't understand what has happened but I'm ready to take him and go on wherever you take us."

After all that had happened, I didn't know even in that moment, there was a dam on the campus that had just broken above us; I had never been told it existed.

# CHAPTER FOUR
## THE STINK WAS EVERYWHERE

Photo: www.DamSafety.org

Our night-clothes were gone. The rushing water was so powerful that it simply tore them off of us, but there in the cab of the truck was a pair of old khaki cut-offs that I put on and wonder of wonders, they fit me! The waters finally receded and we got out of the truck and walked in knee-deep muck and mud, not knowing where we were going. The stink of rotted lake mud, fish, sewer gas, and natural gas, was everywhere.

I got Kirk to a safe place with Paul Stacey and his family, who lived in a trailer on high ground; his house had not even gotten wet. Paul was the chief mechanic for all the vehicles on campus and he welcomed us with open arms. Paul gave me a pair of his work-boots, and with Kirk now settled for the time being, I started the journey--which I did not want to take--the journey of walking the flood-plain; the journey of walking the valley where we lived and played just yesterday.

The flood-plain was now filled with smashed vehicles, pieces of broken homes, and broken splintered trees. It was no longer a place of beauty. And I knew that aside from the great amount of debris lying everywhere, there were probably broken bodies yet to be discovered as well.

The valley was literally strewn with death and destruction. Now I had to start walking in it, hoping to find life, but expecting to find bodies belonging to the rest of my family. Yes, it was a valley full of death and destruction. And even though there were a few people walking about . . . I felt all alone.


## THE STRETCHER IN THE PICK-UP TRUCK

I walked about a half-mile and met some people putting a stretcher into the back of a pick-up truck. Someone had a flashlight and shone it on the face of the woman they were carrying. Her face was purple and green and swollen to the size of a basketball. Her hair was matted about her head like an old sunbonnet, filled with sticks, leaves, and mud.

I said to them, "I think that's Jerry Sproull's wife, but she'll make it to heaven before she ever makes it to the hospital." I had no idea that besides finding my son Kirk, I had also just found another family member. The face I was looking at on the stretcher was the face of my own wife, but I did not recognize her!

I continued to walk, looking and searching under everything; looking for bodies that might be of my own family. I came to a spot where under some river trash and old pieces of houses and limbs from trees, I saw what resembled a body. As I pulled at it I wondered, "Is it a body, or just some old rags and debris? Yes, it is . . . it is a body! God, what if it's one of my kids?"

I was afraid to look, but said to myself, "Doug, you've got to hang on no matter what." As I pulled the body clear and turned it over I said, "No, it's not one of mine, but it is a little boy. I've already found Kirk so it's not him. God bless this little boy. I hope his family will be alright with this. I'll carry him over my shoulder until I find someone that can take him."

I met some rescue workers and they took the little body from my shoulder. I almost hated to let him go. The valley of death was taking many lives that night and I felt helpless.


## LET'S BREAK THE WINDOW

Then I came upon a group of about ten or twelve people in the woods huddled together for warmth. They were wet, tired, dirty, and scared, and one of the ladies said, "I feel as if we've just come through the Valley of Death, and maybe we're in hell."

I recognized the area we were in. It had been the dumping ground for all of our trash. I thought, "Wait a minute! This is just up the hill from Mom and Dad Ronson's house! Maybe it didn't get hit! At least I don't think it did since it was way down over there!"

I shouted to the group, "Hey everybody, listen to me. My Mom and Dad had a house right around the hill from here. If it's still standing we can go there. Anyone want to follow me?" The little band of barefoot survivors moved in behind me as we headed down the hill and around the corner, walking carefully over the debris which was everywhere.

And suddenly, there it was. It didn't even look as if it had been touched. I thought, "Why wasn't I living there instead of where I was? That's the place I wanted to live anyway, instead of on the campus." As we got closer, I saw that it had been knocked about two feet off of its foundation, but it was still standing. It was stable and all in one piece with no apparent, serious damage. I was amazed!

I stepped onto the small porch and found the door locked, which made sense because it had been rented out to two female students who were away on vacation. I decided to break one of the door windows, hoping to reach through to the lock and get us in.

As I raised my fist to break the window I thought, "I hope I don't get cut," but the next thing was, bam! I smashed my fist against the window and it let go with a sharp crack, breaking into pieces. I said to the group, "Unbelievable. That was too easy! And I don't think I cut myself either." I reached in, turned the lock and opened the door. We now had a place to go to.

## HELLO . . . OPERATOR?

I said, "OK everyone. Let's get inside. The beds are dry so let's get the little ones in and get them covered up. Don't worry about their being wet. Just put them in! Sheets will wash later. Get them warm!"

Looking through the rooms I wondered what we could do to get each other comfortable. I came to the closet and said, "Hey, look everyone. There are plenty of clothes in here! Maybe there's enough to get everyone covered up and warm. Just get whatever fits you and we'll worry about how to replace them later. And don't worry that these clothes have belonged to ladies. It looks like there are two sizes here: One for larger ladies and one for smaller ladies. You should find something to work for you. Just get something to put on and take the chill off. Help yourself."

I walked back into the living room while some folks were trying on clothing, and without even realizing what I was doing, I picked up the telephone. I laughed to myself. Of course, there was nothing funny at the moment. We were all shocked by trauma. But now it was like the laughter was in control as it peeled out of me with a foreign sound, disconnected from the seriousness of our situation. It jarred me, and the others looked at me strangely as well.

It was silly to think the telephone would actually work. But as I put the phone to my ear, I was amazed beyond belief to hear the unbelievable buzz of the dial tone! My mind said, "The telephone still has a dial tone! Really? I know it can't be but . . . hey, there is a dial tone? It's working!"

I announced my discovery to the room. The people looked at me, not knowing if I expected them to laugh at my joke, or cry, or ask me if I was delirious, so I said, "Really! I'm not joking! It has a dial tone! Really! I think the telephones are working! Hey . . . really!!"

This had to be the mercy of God because the wall the telephone was mounted on--which was an outside wall--had moved about two feet off of its foundation and should have snapped the wires.

I bellowed, "Hey, who wants to call home?" They looked at me again as if I were crazy. After what had just happened, they weren't ready for a comedian. I saw their doubt and said, "Really. Listen!" I held the phone out into the room away from my ear and this time the buzz was clearly heard by everyone.

We all needed a little hope, and here it was. "Who wants it first? Take turns to let your families know how you are. I don't care how far away they are. Make your long distance calls and I'll take care of the charges later; I'll work it out with the girls who live here. Make them short and quick, though, in case we lose connection." Everyone made calls and then the children were put into beds.

The next thing to be done was to wait; wait for whatever was next.

## FOUR HOURS OF HELL

As I left the house, depression began to hang on to me like a wet blanket. With hope beyond hope, I wanted to find more of my family alive. I went back out, walking through the valley and searching through the wreckage of houses and old buildings, smashed cars, trucks, and trees.

Before long, I found two more bodies. Following that, I took a long ride to the hospital where a temporary morgue had been set up. The station wagon I was in had to travel away from the campus, through town, up the hill, and around the mountain--far above the campus--and then back down the other side of the mountain to approach the hospital. Normally, we would have just gone across the bridge, but it was washed out. So instead of making a trip of three or four blocks, it was a grueling twelve to fifteen-mile trip.

I'm so thankful for the commitment and patience of Professor Norman Allison who drove the many trips in his station wagon, getting all of us to the hospital.

Without him, many things would have been so much harder to deal with that tragic night.

I tried to stretch out on two chairs in the foyer, just wanting to find some rest from the physical pain and the mental exhaustion. It was about 5:30 in the morning and just four hours had passed since the dam broke, but it seemed like an eternity. Even though I knew I couldn't sleep, I longed for something to lie down on and be comfortable, but nothing brought me any relief.

My mind was trying to rest but thoughts of the night's calamities continued whirling through the fogginess of my mind, screaming, "You Failed! Your family is gone! You failed!"

All I could think was, "My God, what a night. No, not a night, but a nightmare! I guess it really did happen. Why? I don't know, but never-the-less, it's true. How I wish this really was only a nightmare. Then I could wake up and it would all be over."

"It's been four hours of hell! Why God? Why? Tell me something! Will I ever know why it happened? What's going to happen next? Will I ever find my family? God, where are they? Please . . . stop this merry-go-round and let me get off."

## THE HALLWAYS BECAME A MORGUE
Daybreak finally came when a nurse approached me and said, "Are you Mr. Veer?" I told her I was, and she said they had found my wife and that she would take me to her. I was shocked.

As I followed the nurse down the maze of hallways I wondered how they kept them so clean, what kind of soap and mop they used, and who did the work. Yes, it was a stupid thought, but at the time--after everything I had just seen and walked through--nothing made sense; I longed for my life to be like these hallways were: clean, uncluttered, and normal. Then I wondered if I would ever have that kind of life again.

Tears began to well up in my eyes and I didn't want to let them out. As we walked farther along, turning left, then right, one hallway after another, I began to see sheet-covered bodies on stretchers and Gurneys, lining the walls of the hallways. As the nurse led me along, I wondered which one of them she would uncover to identify, as the body as my wife.

With that thought in mind, my imagination began running wild as if I were really seeing everything in slow motion. I imagined her lifting up a white sheet, then exposing a lifeless, stark body with a death mask on it. I imagined the nurse facing me to say, "Mr. Veer, here she is."

I walked along in fear, not wanting to see her. I thought, "I've just been through the dirty, wet, muddy valley out there where death is everywhere, and now, here's another valley, but it's a clean, shiny one; clean beyond belief. This long, lonely valley is filled with death also. How long will this continue? Is this a never ending journey through hell, or what? Which one of these bodies will be my wife?"

My thoughts were interrupted as the nurse motioned me into a room. "In here Mr. Veer." I followed her into what looked like an operating room. Hanging from the ceiling were huge, round, concave, mirrored lights above each bed. She took me to one of them which had a woman lying on it and said, "Mr. Veer, is this your wife?"

I walked to the bed and saw a bandage-covered patient. I looked at the face; it was barely recognizable. Relying only on my vision, there was no way I could have possibly identified her.

Never-the-less, my heart which loved her so deeply now was also filled with sorrow for her. On the surface perhaps she was unrecognizable, yet, in my heart, I knew it was her. I was astonished at her condition and simply said, "Yes, this is her."

Admitting this truth broke my heart. She was my beloved, and I knew she was in pain, yet I was so thankful she was alive. Laying there under the huge light she seemed so alone and I wanted to stay by her side and comfort her, but the nurse asked me to leave. Reluctantly I walked away, and as I followed the pathway through the long winding hallways again, I wondered when this would all end. Weeks later, as we talked about that evening in the hospital, she said told me she only saw my love for her as we looked into each other's eyes while I identified her there. She said it was the very encouragement she needed to go on.

## X-RAYS DON'T LIE

After taking 26 x-rays, Toccoa's Stephens County Hospital discovered my wife had a broken, lower left leg, a broken neck, a broken jaw-bone above and below the jaw joints. Also, her lower teeth were jammed into the roof of her mouth, and her face was basically crushed.

She remembered being swept away underneath the raging flood and being caught between a concrete slab and a tree which slowly crushed her body and her face. She remembered the pain was so excruciating that she vomited under the water.

The hospital decided the damage was so serious that they weren't capable of properly taking care of her. So, they packed her in a stretcher with sandbags all around her, and a special pillow of loose sand to support her neck. Then, they put us and the 26 x-rays in an ambulance and transported us forty miles away, to Northeast Georgia Medical Center, in Gainesville, Georgia.

On the way to Gainesville, she tried very hard to talk to me, but it was all guttural mumbling because of the brokenness in her face and jaws. It reminded me of a conversation we had long ago before we ever left Talladega to come to Toccoa. She had been very interested in the life of Joni Eareckson and had written to her a couple of times.

Joni's story was that one summer in 1967 while swimming in a lake--not knowing how shallow it was--Joni dove into the water, breaking her neck, causing permanent paralysis from the neck down. Joni had to be confined to a lifetime of being in a wheelchair.

There in the ambulance, my wife wanted to talk to me about Joni. She kept trying to tell me that she couldn't live month after month, being turned over and over in a Stryker Frame, which is a medical device that holds the patient between two canvas frames, somewhat like the meat in a sandwich. The frame allows the nurses to continually turn one over, changing their position from laying on their front to their back. This helps reduce bedsores.

My wife asked me to pray that she would never have to do this because she knew she would never be able to endure it.

Here's an excerpt from Joni Eareckson's story telling how she felt when she was going through the trauma of her injuries:

"I was lying on a hospital bed in suicidal despair, depressed, discouraged, after the hot July afternoon when I took that dive into shallow water; a dive which resulted in a severe spinal cord injury, which left me paralyzed from the shoulders down, without the use of my hands and my legs.

Before that time, I didn't even know what you called people like me. Who are we? The physically challenged, the mobility impaired, the "differently-abled", handicapped. I knew we weren't crippled or invalid. But I just didn't have any contact with people who were hurting or in pain. That spinal cord injury changed all that.

There I was lying in the hospital bed in the summer of 1967 desperately trying to make ends meet, desperately trying to turn my right side down emotions, right side up. In my pain and despair, I had begged many of my friends to assist me in suicide. That seems to be a common topic these days and many disabled people that I know even in the nineties have a tough time finding life worth living.

I sought to find a final escape, a final solution, through assisted suicide, begging my friends to slit my wrists, dump pills down my throat, anything to end my misery. The source of my depression is understandable. I could not face the prospect of sitting down for the rest of my life without the use of my hands, without the use of my legs. All my hopes seem dashed. My faith was shipwrecked."

All the way to Gainesville, my wife kept mumbling, "I can't live like Joni. I just can't. Pray for me that the only injuries I have will be in my face, not in my body." So I did. Here's another excerpt from Joni's story, in her own words:

Joni continues with her story: "I remember that my hospital bed was situated near a window in the ward that I shared with six other women and I used to thank God that I could see the moon at night and that my room was situated near a tree so I could watch the leaves blow in the wind.

Little things, small things, began to matter. Looking straight on into the eyes of another person in a wheelchair and sensing their pain, being moved by their tears, feeling the rhythm of their heart, sharing oneness in the spirit, and like experiences. These are the things that began to matter to me.

But other things began to matter to me as well. God used this injury to develop patience, endurance, tolerance, self-control, steadfastness, sensitivity, love, and joy. Those things didn't matter much when I was on my feet but, boy, they began to matter after I began living life in a wheelchair.

I began to see that this is what made me a truly peaceful person. This is what real beauty was all about. This is what purpose in life involved, being made somebody special, somebody significant, way down deep on the inside and begin to share that with smiles and encouragement to others."

## WHAT ABOUT THE X-RAYS?

After arriving at Gainesville General Hospital, the technicians looked at the 26 x-rays we brought with us, and my wife was taken to an operating room, which had been made ready ahead of time through a phone call from Stephens County Hospital. Once there, I waited while doctors examined her and discussed her condition. Another round of x-rays was ordered, and I waited breathlessly for the results.

About a half hour later, she was taken to a different floor of the hospital, and a different doctor examined her. She was then assigned to a doctor for the facial injuries; nothing being said about the broken lower leg, the broken arm, the broken ribs, or the broken neck. They all were very busy going about attending to the damage done to her face.

When I finally found someone I could talk to, I managed to ask what they were doing about the other injuries and I was told, "Mr. Veer, we're prepping her right now to be moved and the doctor is waiting to begin work on her facial injuries. If you want to Mr. Veer, you can just follow me."

I wanted to know everything that was going on so I asked him again, "What about the other injuries? When will they start on them? How soon will they get to them?"

He said, "Mr. Veer, her face is already building up some serious infections and we need to get that stopped as soon as possible."

"But what about the other injuries?"

"What other injuries?"

"She has a broken leg, and her neck is broken too and . . . when will they take care of those?"

"Mr. Veer, I don't know of any additional injuries other than various cuts and some serious scrapes, but they will be alright for the time being. Right now, we must address the infection in her face; it's gangrenous. It can't wait. "

I was getting frustrated trying to get through to him. "But there were other injuries showing on the x-rays we brought with us. What about those?"

The person frowned as he looked at me and said, "I don't know what you mean. We have done a thorough examination and have run another complete set of x-rays. They are not showing any other injuries except where her face has been so badly crushed. So please, excuse me now Mr. Veer. I
really do need to go." I stood there confused as he walked down the hall.

## "GOD, I'M JUST A MAN"

Before long we were in a small operating room which looked more like a dentist's office. That's because--to the best of my recollection--a dentist-like chair was the only item in the room, other than a couple of small tables. And there was a halo sort of object above and around my wife's head, which I guessed was for taking ex-rays, but of course, I wasn't sure.

I wished I could have remembered the doctor's name, but everything was so traumatic at the time that now it was gone from my memory. However, the doctor himself will never be forgotten by me. He was marvelous and he put my wife back together again, doing what seemed impossible.

An examination--which I hadn't been part of--determined that gangrene had in fact already started forming in her face, behind the eyes and sinus area. We know that if a person has gangrene it has to be cut out or cut off, or it causes death! Of course, if it were a finger, a hand, a foot, or even a leg, it could be removed, but a head!? No way! But that's where her gangrene was, above the neck, behind the facial structure, and it had to be removed, or else.

Once he had her situated in the operating chair, he went to work removing teeth embedded in all the wrong places and cleaning the debris from her mouth. Perhaps half an hour had passed when I noticed the doctor occasionally pause and stand there with his head down as if trying to figure out his next move. He did this several times.

Finally, he turned and went to the little window in the room, which was about shoulder height. He laid his instruments on the sill and rested his head down upon it. I watched him and wondered what he was doing. Then I realized he had tears falling onto the little window sill and began to lightly sob while he spoke in quiet tones. He said, "God . . . I'm just a man. I can't do this without your help . . . Please help me."

He stood there for a few more minutes, and then quietly went back to his work, cutting a channel through the length of the cheek from bottom to top. He separated the inside flesh from the outside flesh, making it wide enough to pass a surgical tubing through it and up into the gangrenous area so the tube would drain the infection.

He also drilled holes in both of her jaw-bones, until it looked like the holes one would see on a shoe for shoelaces. Finally, he strung silver wires through the holes and wired her jaws together so they would remain closed in order to heal.

He was a marvelous doctor, yet he realized he was only a man; a man who needed God's help to do what he was supposed to do. All of our abilities are limited by our disabilities. But we all have a God to call on who is limitless. That's just what this doctor did, and the surgery was highly successful.


## I DIDN'T WANT TO LOOK

After my wife's surgery was done and they had settled her in a recovery room I went back to Toccoa. Now I needed to find my children. I had to know where they were, what was happening to them, and who was talking care of them.

I arrived at the campus and began asking about them. A security guard told me I needed to go the hospital and ask for a certain nurse. (I have forgotten her name.) So I went back to Toccoa's hospital and found the nurse who said I needed to go with her to identify my daughter. At that time I didn't know which daughter she meant because I had two.

We came to a room full of many Gurneys, each one of them covered with a white sheet. This time I knew what I was going to see. It would be someone from my family who had died and I didn't want to face that truth.

I was told to take my time and be very sure about the identity of the body. I stood there not looking because I didn't know if I could handle it. Finally, I told the nurse I really didn't want to look. She asked, "Is there anyone else who knew her well enough to identify her?" I said I didn't know of anyone, at least not right here and now.

I thought, "If I don't find any of my family here under the sheets, there will still be a chance they've survived. They could still be with someone, somewhere. I just have to wait and find out."

Instead, the nurse lifted the sheet and said, "Is this your daughter Mr. Veer?" I didn't want it to be her, but it was. I wanted to cry but I forced myself to stay controlled enough to say, "Yes, that's my daughter, Jaimée."

I walked away from the Gurney unable to stay in control any longer. Deep shuddering sobs broke from my chest and into my throat making gasping sounds as the tears ran freely down my cheeks. The pain was so great that I don't remember much else for the rest of that day. I just wanted this awful dream to be over. Could it get any worse than this?

# CHAPTER FIVE
## YOU OUGHT TO BE FIRED

I learned that my children were scattered throughout the county staying with various people in three separate places. I didn't know exactly where they were but even if I did, I didn't have a car. I wanted to visit my kids and my wife each day but the long distances to Gainesville, 40 miles away and to the other three areas made travel nearly impossible. I have to say that God came through again.

My friend Tommy Sheriff owned a used car lot. He kindly loaned me a car until we could get our life back in order. I was very grateful and wanted to be considerate as well and not put too many miles on a borrowed car.

The next thing I thought about was my job. Classes couldn't resume until the campus repairs were made. Workers would be needed soon but I didn't have time to take care of that and see my family. Was it my job? Yes, but my first responsibility was to my family.

In the meantime, Roy True--who had been Maintenance Director before me--came back from Texas, voluntarily taking my place. That worked well for about a week. Then I was called into the office of my immediate supervisor who was visibly upset. He asked me, "Where are you spending all your time? You're never here any more ." I tried to explain but he interrupted me.

"You would be better off if you were like Bob Harner and Bill Anderson." That's when I lost it! Bob and Bill both lost their wives when the dam broke. I was angry! Not only because he said that but because he didn't give a flip about the children of those two men. And he didn't give a flip about the two women who died either. His disrespect for them enraged me!

He said, "If you can't take care of your job you ought to be fired, don't you think?" That did it! I was already standing, so without even thinking about it, I reached across the desk and grabbed a handful of the front of his shirt, pulling him from his plush leather chair, and I slammed his head down sideways--cheek down--against the top of his desk. Angrily, I raised my fist in the air. I was going to smash it into his face as hard as I could. I wanted to damage his face like my wife's face had been. Then I stopped.

I stood there for a very long three seconds, (that seemed like five minutes), while I argued with myself about hitting him. Suddenly, I turned him loose, stood up, straightened my shoulders and said, "You know what? You're not worth it! I quit! But just so you get what you deserve, I ought to tell Bob and Bill what you said and let them deal with you. You're a sorry sack of humanity!"

I left the office feeling angry and confused. I thought, "God, haven't we been through enough? What's next? What have we done to deserve this? Why is this happening?"

I walked across the lawn in front of the Administration building. It had not suffered any damage because it had been built on high ground. My mind was spinning and I didn't know how I was going to explain all this to my family.

"Lord, now, what do I do? We really don't have any belongings, so that's not a problem I have to deal with, but what about my family? Where do we go from here?"

## A WALK THROUGH THE VALLEY

Photo: www.Gendisasters.com

I decided to take a walk through the valley to see what was left of the place we once lived. There were a few other people walking around quietly too, with their heads cast downward, seeming to be in somewhat of a daze. Even though there was an English teacher walking with me she was deep in her own thoughts, so I thought I probably looked just like she and everyone else did.

Nothing meant much to me anymore except my family. As I walked I would occasionally kick something out of my path. Sometimes I'd pick up an object, look at it, then throw it back. I saw a small black plastic purse. I picked it up and opened it. I was shocked! To my amazement, it had a picture of my daughter Jaimée inside! Then I remembered it was a plaything of hers. Of course, it was wet, but not too dirty and the picture was in pretty good shape. I held it gently, close to my chest as if it were actually her.


## MEDIA LIES

As I continued walking, I picked up a swollen, dirty book. The title, "Sermon on the Mount" told me it was one of mine. I had been reading it recently, but I knew it could never be read again so I casually threw it into the now peacefully flowing creek. It was just a thoughtless gesture but apparently, there was a news reporter nearby who saw me and erroneously reported, "One of the students walking hand in hand with a woman friend found a Bible. He seemed to be angry with God, as he looked at it and then violently threw it into the water."

Nothing could have been further from the truth. The "Bible" as he called it was just a book, swollen beyond the hope of being read again. The "woman friend" was--as I said--one of the English teachers simply offering company to a survivor; nothing else. And there was no hand-in-hand walking.

Many stories came from reporters wanting to dramatize everything to make a name for themselves and make as much money as they could from the suffering of others. I mean, some of the reporters were extremely rude and thoughtless, but then, I guess they were trying to get the best story they could, for their own use. In some cases, it would be at our expense. Perhaps if they had to walk the same emotionally distraught valley I was walking through they would have acted differently.

## EVERYTHING HAS AN END

I continued walking, all the way to the place which used to be our trash dumping site. That's the place I had met with the small group of folks just hours before and took them to Mom and Dad Ronson's house. It happened just a few hours ago but it seemed more like a lifetime ago. I guess I was in a daze still wanting for none of this to be true.

Over in a pile of debris and tall grass near a tree, something colorful caught my eye. I walked toward it and pulled away some of the mud surrounding it; just enough to see what it was. To my surprise, it was a colorful little bright yellow, white and red push toy called a "corn popper". was pushed across the floor.

Photo: www.DamSafety.org

It had a large clear ball filled with small colored balls that would pop and jump as it The handle was gone but I recognized it as a toy belonging to my daughter Jaimée who had died.

Without picking it up I simply stared at it thinking, "Yes, everything has an end and I guess there's a time to let go, no matter what it is, no matter how much it hurts. I hope I'm strong enough to do that."

## I JUST WANTED TO GO HOME

My whole world was turned upside-down. I was like a thirsty man wandering in a desert. I was confused and worried and lost all ability to make decisions. I had no one to lean on or look to for advice.

That first night, God sent a couple to comfort me. They worked at the College. Ken Sanders and his wife Helen took me in for a meal and I fell asleep on their sofa. It was the first real rest I had since the dam broke on us. I'll always be thankful for their thoughtful love and kindness, at a time when it was needed most.

Several days later when my wife was released from the hospital and we were provided with some rooms at the Toccoa Motel. The accommodations weren't the best in town, but at least we had beds and warmth. About a week later the Department of Housing and Urban Development, also known as HUD, purchased a vacant lot in town and set up twenty older mobile homes for some of the survivors to move into. Again, it wasn't the best, but after having lost everything we were thankful to have a place to call home.

During that first week or so after surviving the dam-break I ran into a student who had been at the College for a couple of years. He was interested in what had happened to us so we talked. I told him about the eery train I thought I saw that night when I looked out of my bedroom window.

He told me there was an old wooden dormitory on campus no longer being used except for storage. It was floating on the five-foot crest of water which came first and behind that was the fifty-foot crest which was released when the dam let go completely. In the darkness, its image roughly took on the shape of a train engine followed by the long smooth tops of passenger cars.

That's when I really learned about the dam and how poorly it had been maintained and how the Army Corps of Engineers had already given written warning of its poor condition.

Photo: www.GenDisasters.com

As Director of Campus Maintenance, I should have been made aware of that, but I wasn't. I guess it wouldn't have made too much difference anyway because after twenty years without being maintained, it was so eroded its failure was eminent.

## WHEN A BARGAIN IS NOT A BARGAIN

We moved into one of the mobile homes provided by HUD. The agreement was that if we lived in the mobile home for a period of one year we could purchase it for one dollar. That would have been a bargain, but we were still trying to work through all our emotional pain from the dam-break.

Typically, in most older mobile homes, the heater is built into the wall in the hallway. Of course, night time was the hardest for us, since that's when the dam-break occurred, but it became even worse whenever the blower motor for the heater would kick on and cause a noise that sounded like the roar of rushing water. The sound put us in the midst of that same terror in our minds. It was like the roar of the water screaming at us, ready to destroy everything all over again and take our lives. We had to relive it over and over, nearly every night. And someone would always wake up and cry out for help.

I seriously wondered when it all would end. What I really wanted was to go home to the way things were. But the fear we carried from the "valley of death" might follow us for years to come. Even now, I sometimes have thoughts or dreams which seem to weaken all of those old feelings. Back then, we were troubled every night, but thankfully help came, although it was from an unexpected source.

## PLEASE, SING ME TO SLEEP

Jerry Nicholson, his wife Pat, and their twin boys were survivors just like us. They had a trailer next to ours, also given to them by HUD. Actually, the giving of money and gifts became a way of life for us survivors. We were trying to help each other find our way back to normalcy. We did such things without thinking, and we were driven to being kind and supportive of one another. Jerry and Pat were no exception.

One afternoon Jerry came over and gave us a small record player. It wasn't expensive. It had a kind of pressed-board case that a child's model might have. Even so, it was given from a survivor's heart. They also gave us a couple of records with the record player and they became the real blessing.

I don't think Jerry knew about our night-time dilemma, but what he gave us was perfect for our need. One of the records was of Kenneth Copeland singing "Ye Are a Chosen Generation". His song would calm us and minister to us when we woke to that awful sound of the heater in the middle of the night. Without it, I don't know how we would have made it those first few weeks.

Here is part of that song, written from a Bible passage in First Peter 2:9-10, which says,

*But ye are a chosen generation, a royal priesthood,*
*an holy nation, a peculiar people;*
*that ye should shew forth the praises of Him*
*who hath called you out of darkness*
*into his marvelous light;*
*which in time past were not a people,*
*but are now the people of God:*
*which had not obtained mercy,*
*but now have obtained mercy.*

How those words lifted us I can't begin to tell you. To be told that we are chosen, to be considered royal, and to be called Holy, is more than anyone deserves. True. But those last five words especially comforted us in our very real time of doubt and grief. The words, *"but now have obtained mercy"* became a cornerstone if you will, on which we could plant all our fears and feelings, as we went on struggling. Yes, struggling, with our damaged lives. But we went on knowing we were in His mercy, and we needed that.

## MOSES IN THE BUSHES

One day while in town I met a student who worked at J. C. Penny. She told me she had been approached by a young man who asked, "Excuse me but aren't you one of 'the Falls kids?'" She said she was. He asked, "Do you happen to know the Veers?" She told him she knew us and he said he wanted her to give us a message for him. She agreed.

He went on. "I'm the one who found their daughter Jaimée that next morning. I was with a group looking for bodies when I saw this doll lying in the bushes so I went to look at it. When I got to it I saw it wasn't a doll; it was a baby. She was on her side, asleep, with her hands folded under her cheek. It reminded me of a story I remembered from when I was a little boy in Sunday school. The story was about a baby who was hidden in a basket and sent down the river that his life might be saved. The basket got caught in some bushes, just like this little girl had been that morning. I was so happy to find her but when I bent down to pick her up, I saw that she was dead. I'm so sorry . . ."

He continued. "Well what I'd like you to tell them is when I picked her up and held her in my arms, she seemed to be smiling at me. She was so beautiful that I felt like I was looking into the face of God. I hadn't been to church in a long time, but I'm going now, every time the doors open. I don't know yet what it is, but you folks at 'the Falls' have something special and I want to have it too."


## NO BASKET

I still remember what it was like to be caught in that nether world of water instead of this oxygen rich world of air that sustains us. I've often wondered what it was like for my daughter, Jaimée in those last moments of her life as she was robbed of her breath. I have imagined her fear and pain during that awful night, in that terrible hour. Those moments must have been terrifying for her because she couldn't understand what was happening as she drew her last watery breath in her own valley of death.

I find peace, though, in what her mother so comfortingly said: "Perhaps God in His kind mercy took Jaimée that night while she was still asleep in my arms, lying next to me in the bed where she had just been nursed."

Passing through the portal of death takes only a brief moment explains the Apostle Paul. Furthermore, he said in Second Corinthians 5:8: ". . . to be absent from the body [is] to be present with the Lord," (NKJV).

My belief in God's Word assures me that because of the unblemished purity of an innocent child, God in His infinite mercy took Jaimée home to be with Him.  He took her even before she was ever wrapped in the wildly raging 55 foot high, 110 mile per hour rushing water of the Toccoa Falls River that descended over a 186 foot water fall.

If it were not for God's goodness, insanity would have set in for us. But the God of this universe is One of love and mercy. He loved us so much that He gave Jesus, His own child, to die for us that we might have peace.

Jesus said, *""I leave you peace. It is my own peace I give you. I give you peace in a different way than the world does. So don't be troubled. Don't be afraid. You heard me say to you, `I am leaving, but I will come back to you.' If you loved me, you would be happy that I am going back to the Father, because the Father is greater than I am,"* (John 14:27, 28 ERV).

Yes, there was a flowing river, and there were bushes and trees, but there was no basket for our daughter, Jaimée. There were just the loving arms of a mother to guide her into the presence of God.

I rejoice because this isn't the end of being with our little one. One day we'll be with her again, in heavenly places. All this will be forgotten; our tears will all be wiped away because in heaven, *". . . there shall be no more death, nor sorrow, nor crying. There shall be no more pain . . ."* (Revelation 21:4 NKJV). And Isaiah tells us *". . . a little child shall lead them,"* (Isaiah 11:6 NKJV). Oh, how I look forward to that day!

Photo: www.MarieLetsEat.com

## WE ALL HAVE TO EAT

In the middle of Toccoa, on Big-A Road, there was a restaurant called Bell's Drive-in. Although it had been a drive-in for many years in the past, it still has a walk-up window where you can order, get your food, and sit outside to eat. There is also plenty of seating inside. It's a very homey place so if you feel like sitting down to eat a meal, this would be the place to do it.

In those tender first few days following the dam-break, we would wander from place to place trying to figure out where to eat. I would pull up to a curb, or sit in a parking lot, trying to decide where to go. Many times we drove from place to place, covering nearly every eating place in town, but would never get out of the car. We would just sit in the car and cry. Cry? Yes, because of being incapable of making a decision.

Even though we stopped at every place that served food, we would go without a meal because we were still so filled with trauma. I know that may sound crazy to you, but it's how we lived for many weeks, and if you've never been there, don't even try to understand it. You won't be able to. One thing is for certain though. No matter how much our emotions controlled us, or how many tears we cried, we still had to eat to stay alive.


## FEED HER LIKE A MOMMA BIRD
My wife had undergone several operations because of the injuries to her face. Her jaws were now wired together and she was missing a few molar teeth on each side which left a gap. But even if she could have opened her mouth enough to take in food, she could never have chewed it. So when we did get something to eat, I would take her food into my mouth, chew it, and then pass it back to her through the small opening in her mouth. It was like a mother bird feeding her young.

Of course, during that time, she was able to use a straw to drink liquids. But eating was tough for her. I guess it was a test of survival, and this is what we did because this is how we needed to survive.

One day, we parked at Bells Drive-in, which is where we had parked many times before. Again, we sat in the car and cried. After several moments though, we actually got out of the car and went inside. And unless I'm badly mistaken it was Thanksgiving day, which would have been just nineteen days after the dam-break. We badly needed to break the cycle of not knowing where to eat or how to act like normal people at mealtime.

I don't remember what we ordered, but I do remember the food was delicious! We must have sat there for over an hour just because we were enjoying it so much and also because of my chewing food like a mother bird and passing it through to the mouth of my wife. When we finally decided we may have over-stayed our welcome, (taking up a table that other customers could be using), we got up to leave.

## CALLED INTO THE OFFICE

As I walked toward the cashier near the front door, I asked the waitress for our ticket. Her reply was, "Mr. Veer, you'll have to see Mr. Bell about that." Immediately, a chill of concern swept over me, thinking we had done something wrong. Living in a state of trauma puts you in a place where anything out of the ordinary causes a kind of panic to pass over you. I thought maybe we had stayed too long at the table.

I stuttered a minute trying to gather my wits but I wasn't getting anywhere very fast. The waitress said, "Mr. Bell would like to see you in his office. I'll take you there." Now I knew we were in trouble. We made our way to the back of the restaurant and down a short passage to the office. There was Mr. Bell at his desk. The waitress introduced us and left. My knees were shaking and I thought we were in trouble for the way we were eating, passing food from my mouth to my wife's mouth. I couldn't think of any other reason why he'd be upset at us.

Mr. Bell extended his hand and as I took it he said, "Mr. Veer; Mrs. Veer. I'm so glad to finally meet you." I was surprised! I couldn't understand why he would say that. He went on to say,

"Mr. Veer, I know what you folks have been through. I know you lost your precious little girl, Jaimée, and I know your world has been turned upside-down. I also know you're living in a motel where you can't fix a decent meal. I hope you enjoyed yourself here today and I hope you'll come back again many times. But, Mr. Veer, your money is no good in this restaurant. I've never been through anything like what you're going through, but in the best Christian way I know how, I hope to show you that I'm very sorry for your loss and that my sympathies and prayers will be with you. Thank you so much for coming here to eat with us."

I was flabbergasted! Tears had welled up in my eyes and I couldn't find the words to thank him. I guess I made it through with some sort of verbal mumbling because before I knew it we were outside and in the car. I sat in the car--dumbstruck--over the amount of information he had about us. He knew our names, where we were living, and even the fact we had lost a daughter. The shocking part is that he even knew her name. I was amazed that someone who wasn't from the College would be so caring and so interested in us. What a special man he was.

## WE CAN'T EAT HERE ANYMORE

During the next couple of months, we ate at Bell's quite often, and Mr. Bell would never let us pay the bill. Then, one day as we were leaving, I went back into the office and said to him, "Look, Mr. Bell, I really appreciate what you've been doing for us, but, I'm going to have to quit eating here." With a shocked look on his face he said, "But why? What's wrong? Have we offended you in any way?"

"No, Mr. Bell," I said, "it isn't that, but I feel as if we're sponging off of you, taking advantage of your kindness, and generosity. I just can't do that anymore. It's not fair to you." He replied,

"Alright Mr. Veer, I'll tell you what we'll do. First of all, you call me Jimmie. That's my name. And you keep coming here and let me continue having you as my guest. And then, at the end of February, you can start taking care of the check. Is that okay?" I agreed and we enjoyed many more meals there. Even more so, we were blessed to enjoy his wonderful friendship.

Jimmie Bell is one of those special people whom I'll never forget. Not because he fed us food, but because he fed us with the sort of love and kindness which we so desperately needed at that time to feel comforted, and to feel as if we were really alive. He made a genuine attempt to understand our needs at a time when nothing in our world was stable and he showed us that we would be able to put life back together when we weren't sure we ever could. I'll never forget Jimmie Bell of Bell's Drive-in Restaurant in Toccoa, Georgia. Of all my Toccoa dam-break experiences, he will forever be one of the brightest memories I'll keep.

# CHAPTER SIX
## WE'VE LOST THAT LOVIN' FEELING

During the weeks, months, and years, following the dam-break, our marriage became even more volatile than the powerful, destructive waters we had come through. Instead of being drawn closer together by what we had just experienced, I found we were having arguments more often than we had in the past and they would never seem to be resolved. Although my surviving family became the center of my universe, it seemed as though more and more the deep despair we were living in caused my wife to draw up into a world that revolved around herself. It was a world filled with depression that I guess she hoped would shut out the anguish we were trying to recover from.

The more I was drawn to the importance of family, the more she pulled away from me, as if she had a fear of believing that family could ever again be a loving, safe haven. Perhaps the loss we experienced was too great to carry and from there, everything about our family unit went down hill.

I tried to get on with our life but I felt she hated me in spite of it. I worked hard and made a good living for us, buying houses, land, and rental properties, but it was never enough. She was always on the move for something new, searching for something to crowd out the memories and take her to a "new place" to find the "old life" we used to have. But that was torn away from us in the darkness of that November night.

In retrospect, if I were to make a comparison between the dam-break experience and the aftermath it would be like this: The bitterness, anger, and loss, I had because of what we went through *after* the dam-break is like a huge mountain; the actual dam-break experience is a like a mole-hill.

I don't mean to minimize the horror of that terrible night, but by comparison, immediate death in the flood waters may have been more merciful. In my view, the distress that came to us, our children and our marriage is by comparison, astronomical.

The hurt was bigger than the many tons of rock and debris brought down on us; it was greater than the millions of gallons of water screaming forth and unbridled over the waterfall and down through the valley. The brokenness of the marriage and family bond was so much more damaging. But the effects of both will be carried forward into the future for all who have survived. We will all bear the scars forever.

## UNTOLD STORIES

There are many untold stories of the survivors and their families, which will never be known. The autumn cold that penetrated our flesh that fatal night has crept into many other marriages as well. Those ties have been broken and as much loss has been experienced as the loss the rushing waters stole from us, materially.

For us, there was no longer any marital trust. I got to the place where all I could think was "I don't trust you." Perhaps her problems actually resulted from losing Jaimée.

At the same time, several other lives were destroyed that were not recorded in the book, *Dam-Break in Georgia*. My surviving children suffered because of the dam-break. Even the lives of my two precious daughters we had following the dam-break were affected.

Because of these problems (which could have been lessened with counseling) I really do have a hard time now extending trust to anyone; especially women, and more especially, wives!

Please understand, I love and respect woman, but I feel as though once they becoming legally married, the marriage license becomes a "license to kill". That's right. I feel like many of them by becoming a wife, take a license to kill love, to kill kindness, to kill honesty, and to kill trust; especially trust.

I'm not being chauvinistic, but I do feel as though men are more open, simpler, and easier to understand. Women, by and large, are closed, deceptive, and selfish. I wish I didn't feel this way. Perhaps that's another set of emotions I still have to deal with.


**ETCHED IN MY MEMORY**

December 7, 1941, Pear Harbor was bombed by the Japanese in a deadly attack which was never foreseen. Likewise--regarding the night of November 6, 1977--I hereby take the freedom to speak the same words as did President Franklin D. Roosevelt in his speech to the Joint Session of Congress just after Pearl Harbor was bombed:

"This is a day that will live in infamy . . .
Very many lives have been lost.
Gentlemen, this is a day we will always remember
. . . and they shall never forget."

I wish in our case, these words would have been true: that the College would have never forgotten us, but they have. Only those who survived, and our loved ones and families remember that night because those in authority at the College seem to have long erased their memory of us.

As a matter of fact, after my wife had her broken face put back together in Gainesville, Georgia, by that wonderful surgeon, he said the procedure would have to be redone in two years. I guess it was a case of fine tuning the work as everything grew back into place.

When we approached the College two years later to have the surgery done, the presiding President of the College told me, "We have erased the blackboard of our responsibilities for that night. We no longer owe you anything."

While we, the survivors, continue to remember and mourn that terrifying night, which by-the-way literally saved the college from going under financially, we have become just a dim, distant memory in their past. The truth is, instead of imminent bankruptcy due at the end of that year, such was avoided because of money from the government and donations from caring people around the world. But we the victims of the dam-break paid the price. Now we were both unremembered and unappreciated.

We who have lost friends and loved ones dear to us, and yet have survived, will never forget that we were left adrift in a corrupt sea of political greed by the college's governing body at that time. Our Commander in Chief (the College President) seemed to have no caring for our suffering and sorrows or our emotional and financial needs. The truth is, his own son, a student there, had great compassion for us and did not appreciate the attitudes of the administration.

As a matter of fact, a large portrait of one of the administrators was taken from the admin building wall and was hidden for several days as an act of protest over how the survivors were being treated. It was found some time later on the roof of that same building. Hmm. I wonder who might have done that?

## MONEY BEFORE MARRIAGES

We were set adrift alright, just as surely as if we had never made it out of the raging waters. For the survivors, it was truly a day that would live in infamy; always to be remembered; never to be forgotten. As survivors, we haven't stayed closely in touch, yet we are like a ghost family. We are always connected in memory, in experience, and in understanding, even if not in person. Our feelings and love for one another never have, and never will die off into the past.

On the other hand, it seems as though Toccoa Falls College has elected to forget us, violating the trust we had in them, not only as our educators, but also as our guides, protectors, and spiritual examples. The violation of that trust has hurt us nearly as much as our personal losses have.

Again I would say that the loss of many innocent lives have paid the price and paved the way for the college. It kept them from locking their doors due to bankruptcy. Cash, checks, and pledges flowed like swift waters, into the financial well of the college, providing the money needed to remain open. Just as the flood waters slowly receded from the campus, so every ounce of decency also drained away from those in charge of the finances. They had a physical cash flow but they were morally bankrupt. Their desire to use donation funds for their own purposes was greater than the desire to honor those well-meaning, compassionate people, whose intent was to help the survivors rebuild their lives.

Some administrators may have considered the few dollars designated to survivors as an acceptable recompense for the loss of thirty-nine lives, but that wasn't even close to a down payment. Perhaps a price can be put on the death of a loved one, but what price can be put on the death of a marriage or the well-being of a family? Why do I include the well being of a family? Because for those couples who survived the dam-break, there were many divorces that followed, thus killing the family structure for the children who would be affected the for rest of their lives.

## I DARE YOU!

I remember that the physical clean up hadn't even started when as quickly as the very next day, trauma counselors came from as far away as New York to help the survivors. They offered their services at no charge. They wanted to help us understand how to cope with the traumatic aftermath and the emotional pain.

Classes soon resumed and one day during a chapel service, the President of the College addressed the student body. He issued a challenge to all of the survivors as follows: He said, "I dare you! I dare you to go to a psychologist for counseling and *still* call yourself a Christian!" I have that on tape, just as I recorded it from that service. Let me explain:

Two weeks prior, on a Saturday morning, my daughter, Jaimée, and I had been in our back yard picking small yellow daisies. We went inside the house, (I think it was about lunch time), and took some of the flowers with us. As we talked and played together, Jaimée had climbed up onto the table to reach for the flowers. We engaged a small tape recorder to catch some of her first words.

One of the things she would do, (which we loved so much), was to squint her left eye with a sort of a

*Popeye-the-Sailor-Man* expression and say, "N-n-n-nope!" and we all would laugh.

The following week we sent that recording to Talledega, to our somewhat adoptive Mom and Dad who were pastoring our former church there, the Christian and Missionary Alliance.

Shortly after the dam-break, we got the tape back. We used the same tape to record the college President's statement: "I dare you to seek help through counseling." The tape verifies what he said, and to this day it's still in our possession.

Ironically, the college now offers courses in counseling. Yes, times have changed but that doesn't alleviate the harm that was done to those who couldn't receive counseling because it may have cast a shadow of doubt on their salvation.


## WATERS GONE WILD

On that Saturday night/Sunday morning, as the dam broke, we were upset by the events that came upon us. The waters had gone wild and deep into our spirits, but we found the unbounded courage and unfathomable desire to survive for the sakes of our loved ones. We had a *want-to* sort of outlook as we all pulled together to go on, even in the midst of our grief.

As survivors of the dam-break at Toccoa Falls College, we have never been treated fairly by the administration. In spite of that, we have been made stronger by the memories of our loved ones who were swept away by the waters; those memories are deeper than the waters that flowed over us. Were we fairly compensated for our losses? No. But we have the riches of love, one for another, that will never fade, no matter how much of it we spend. It's an eternal bond of shared survival that flows through every one of us who survived that awful, terrible night . . . which could have been prevented.

Oh, did I just say it could have been prevented? Yes. There were reports by the Army Corps of Engineers that warned of the possibilities of the dam erupting, but they went unheeded. Such little attention was paid to that warning, that as I was being oriented for my job, taking on the responsibilities of Director of the physical plant of the College--all 1100 acres--I was never told of the existence of a dam on the campus property.

## WELCOME THE NEW GENERATION

Have I had bitterness toward Toccoa Falls College? Yes. At first I didn't because we were in such shock. We were just trying to deal with immediate needs and the everyday survival of the moment. But bitterness became my only way of dealing with the mixed emotions I had in the following years. The bitterness came through our knowing we had paid the ultimate price for the college to recover. Bitterness came because the college had benefitted, had the dam not broken. And it came because of how we had been treated by the past administration. Ever since then, we've been trying to heal from our losses. They, on the other hand, have found healing for their financial woes.

I have to say that I am also thankful. Through the years, I've met and come to intimately know some of those blessed folks who have come through the attractive entrance to the school. I'm sure they probably felt as thrilled as I did years earlier while driving past the long, curved, white stone wall displaying the words, "Where Character Is Developed

With Intellect". I can only wish that those in authority back on November 1977 would have adhered to, and embraced those words. Had they embraced those words personally, their own character traits would have been shaped as well. The end result for the survivors may have been far different than the pain we have had to live with following that disastrous November night.

## AND THE PAIN GOES ON

I've not been able to keep in touch with most of those who survived. So many of us have gone our separate ways. Some, back to where their families were, some, back to where they previously once lived, some, went on to find a new place to reside where it was hoped that sanity and peace might be found.

From time to time I've heard various reports about some of their lives. Unfortunately, much of it was unpleasant. The hopes and dreams they brought with them to Toccoa Falls had been dashed. They had been pushed out of the way like the boulders that came over the waterfall that night, bringing an unbelievable torrent of affliction, brushing aside trees and houses like toys on a child's playroom floor.

I know of only one marriage that didn't end in divorce, remaining intact a few years after the dam-break. It was the union of Pat and Jerry Nicholson. They and their twin boys made it out alive, together. I pray they are still a solid thriving family. But many surviving husbands and wives who lost a loved one also lost their marriage. How sad is that?

Harriett Schiff, who was a journalist for the Detroit Free Press in the 1960s, wrote a book titled The Bereaved Parent. Her writing addresses several effects on a marriage caused by the loss of a child.

She reports that according to statistics, 75% to 95% of marriages will come to an end after a child's death. She adds that this study may not represent a reliable scientific statistic but she did say that the death of a child absolutely creates stressors in a marriage that warrant extra support and counseling for parents in such situations. Please remember her statement:"The death of a child creates stressors in a marriage, and those families need extra support and counseling after the death of a child"

Also consider that men and women grieve differently; therefore, they will cope differently with their loss. Schiff concludes by asking a major question, "How will they eventually find healing from the trauma if they can not bear their pain alone?"


## SPOKEN FROM MY HEART

While we were still in Toccoa, trying to put our life back together, someone gave us a book of poetry. In that book, I found this poem by Violet Storey. She speaks so much better for me than I could for myself, and puts into words what I'd like to say to God about my precious little angel, Jaimée.

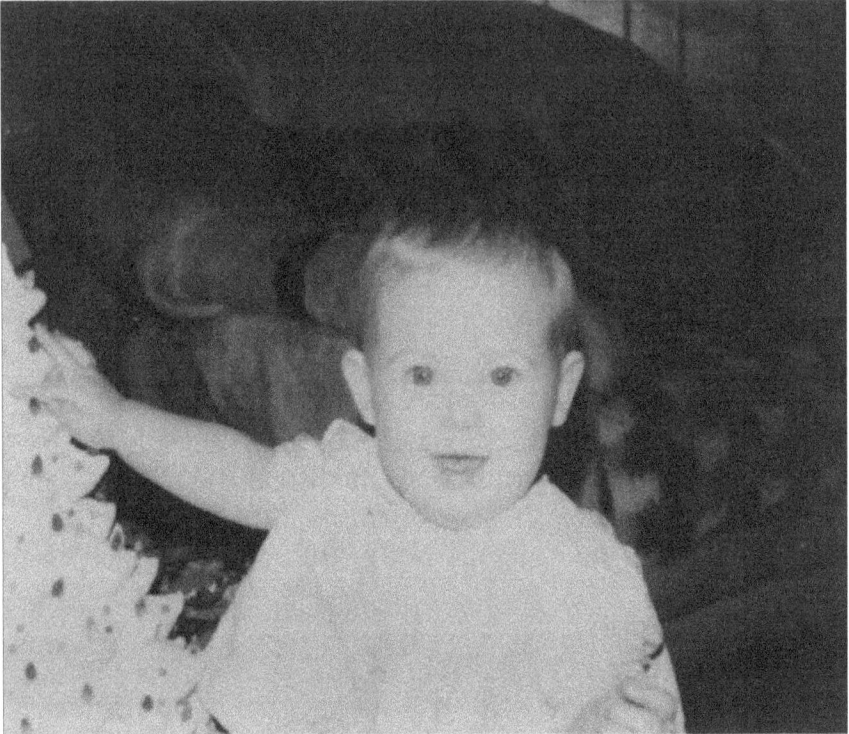

Photo: Douglas Veer

## Prayer for a Very New Angel
### By Violet Alleyn Storey

God, God, be lenient her first night there.
The crib she slept in was so near my bed;
Her blue-and-white wool blanket was so soft,
Her pillow hollowed so to fit her head.

Teach me that she'll not want small rooms or me
When she has You and Heaven's immensity!
I always left a light out in the hall.
I hoped to make her fearless in the dark;

And yet, she was so small-one little light,
Not in the room, it scarcely mattered. Hark!
No, no; she seldom cried! God, not too far
For her to see, this first night, light a star!

And in the morning, when she first woke up,
I always kissed her on her left cheek where
The dimple was. And oh, I wet the brush.
It make it easier to curl her hair.

Just, just tomorrow morning, God, I pray,
When she wakes up, do things for her my way!

*My precious daughter Jaimée Suzanne Veer*
*2-13-76 to 11-06-77*


## THE DAMAGING DARE!

I had mentioned earlier how counselors had come to help us with our grief. We could have benefitted from such counseling but we were threatened by the College President's statement, "I dare you to ask for counseling and *still* call yourself a Christian!" Had we accepted the counseling and been supported instead of being challenged, our healing could have come and the lives of surviving families would have been strengthened rather than destroyed, as many of them were. Can you sense my anger here? They refused the needed services that caused unnecessary losses *after* the dam-break, not to mention their glaring mismanagement of funds.

The callous challenge caused many unnecessary divorces and painfully broken homes which could have been prevented. Maybe the nightmares could have been prevented too. And not only has it been damaging to the children who survived, but also to the children who would later be born into those marriages. Yes, I am angry, although I feel it is righteous anger on my part and for that I make no apology.

Let me put it another way. In the months following that chilled wintry night when the dam broke, the valley of peace was strewn with thirty-nine unnecessary deaths. Many marriages saw their final days. And the real cause of my anger is due to the great sorrow that has fallen upon the children of those broken homes.

At the same time, it has been *business-as-usual* for the college. They go peacefully, productively, and forgetfully on their merry way. Yes, that is an anger I have not yet been able to resolve.

The College is still there, the waterfall is still there, the creek is still there, but for many husbands and wives who physically survived together, now their marriages are gone. They could have been helped, but all that is passed and the opportunity is no longer available; all because of a thoughtless, ignorant dare! Isn't it strange that today, the College now offers courses and degrees in psychology and Christian counseling?

## THE NEXT FIVE YEARS

We left Toccoa after the dam-break. The pain was great and the memories were constant. We were called to minister at a Christian and Missionary Alliance Church in Tuscaloosa, Alabama, and we were glad to leave Toccoa behind. But could we run away from the emotional damage and the memories?

After spending a couple of years in Tuscaloosa, we were called to another church, this time in Columbus, Mississippi. While we were there, I also went back to work for the Daniel Construction

Company, building hi-rises. I spent another few years there, and then we moved back to Toccoa, Georgia. It seemed as if we were spinning around in the circle again.

I still hoped that we could find the marriage we lost five years before, but it did not happen. My wife moved to Pittsburgh, Pennsylvania and as Paul Harvey would say, "That's another story." Unfortunately, separation and divorce did come, although it was not unexpected.

Twelve years later I met and married another student, Kathy Frost. Kathy came to Toccoa Falls from Canada; she was pursuing a degree in psychology and Christian counseling. She graduated with honors. Less than a year later we were married. As of 2017, we've been married twenty years. The peace in our marriage is wonderful.


## NEW BLOSSOMS ON THE TREE OF LIFE

I've been back to the College a few times. The mud has dried, and there's a healthy blanket of grass covering the fear-soaked landscape that had swallowed so many of us that night. I take it as a declaration that life must go on.

The dirty, broken, remnants of twisted automobiles and homes have all been carried away and buried. Streets, bridges, and buildings have all been repaired, and new ones now stand where once those November waters raged, fifty-five feet high, destroying everything in its path. The flood plain is dry but not all the tears have dried from our faces.

The valley once again looks peaceful, and I am thankful for that. Thankful, because now as I walk upon the valley's flood-plain, the terror of it is no longer visible, except in our own minds. The Valley of

Death, which my mind knows so well, has now become a Valley of Hope for those who have and will come to find blossoms of a new life for them and their loved ones.

The Valley of Death of November 6, 1977 has now become a symbol of how as survivors, we paid the ultimate price giving the college *life after death*. And for the many students who have attended there since that time, I am so grateful. I wish them all the blessings of educational, spiritual, and moral growth their lives can absorb.

Photo: www.TFCHistory.com

These new students, teachers, and administrators have no debt to pay in this aftermath. I'm so thankful for that and for the continuing education at Toccoa Falls College. I hope it will be a place where people will find their rainbow and a strong bridge that opens the way to new, productive lives. May God bless each and every one of them.

# CHAPTER SEVEN
## SHORT STORIES

So, the years have rolled along and I'm left with many memories. I've told you some of the sad ones, the painful ones, the ones that still tear at my emotions, and I've shared a few that I'll probably never get over. But now I'd like to share some things that you might find interesting.

As the word of the tragedy at Toccoa Falls College began to hit the news, it spread like wild-fire. The book, *Dam Break in Georgia*, was published in record time. Hardly had the mud dried in the valley when the book hit the marketplace. Also, the news media spread it like lightening, not only in the United States but across the globe!

## A PHONE CALL

While my wife was in the hospital in Gainesville Georgia, after the surgery on her face, we received a long distance phone call in the hospital room. There were no cell phones then. A nurse came in and had the phone call transferred to her bedside. It was from Germany! The person on the other end said, "We just heard of your tragedy and loss, and we want you to know that we are Christians. We are part of the body of Christ just as you are and when one part hurts we all hurt. We love you and will hold on to you in prayer."

After that, my wife prayed that she would be released from the hospital to be able to attend the funeral but her injuries were too serious. Even so, God's goodness overwhelms us sometimes, as it did this time. The funeral was televised and close-ups of my daughter's casket could be seen. In essence my wife was able to be at the funeral via the television screen. Yes, God *is* good.

In the meantime a procession of three or four cars were on their way to Toccoa from Freeport, Illinois, and from Martin, Tennessee. Family members formed a caravan, and were on their way to see us in the hospital in Gainesville, Georgia. They brought with them lots of joy and comfort.

Our family has always been close knit. Even so, their arrival was a true surprise to us. Love has always been the substance that has bonded us together. That love was taught and received from our terrific mother and father. Yes, through all our turmoil and tragedies our family has been blessed.

Another blessing was that Joe Teel who had worked with me in Childersburg, Alabama on those high buildings, heard about the dam-break and the funerals. Joe made the trip from Alabama to Toccoa, Georgia just to attend the funeral of my daughter Jaimée and to be a support to me.

That's a friend that sticks closer than a brother as we're told in Proverbs 18:24. Although Joe didn't even get to talk to me, he was at the funeral and saw the whole thing first hand, not on television. Thank you Joe, my Christian brother; my friend.


## A PIGGY BANK

Young twin boys in South Dakota, also contacted us to say they had broken into their piggy bank and had wrapped all the pennies, nickels, and dimes. They sent them to us with a note saying, "We just want to help you." How precious to see the compassion in these tender children.

## LAST DOLLAR

A young man in jail in North Carolina was given a copy of the *Dam Break* book. After he read it he said he knelt by the bunk in his cell and asked God how he could help us. Then, he wrote us a short letter telling us how he grieved for us and sent us his last dollar. He said, "I have a warm place to live and food to eat. You don't. So although this is my last dollar, I'm sending it to you because I know you need it more than I do."

## WHY DID HE DO THAT?

Right after the dam-break, we went back to Talladega, Alabama for a short visit, just for the weekend. That weekend I ran into Eric, a man I had known before we left there to go to Toccoa. Eric either owned or worked at Belks clothing store and we often saw each other around town and in restaurants.

As we talked about what I had just been through Eric said, "Doug, I thought God was supposed to be all about love. So, why did he allow 39 of his own Christian people to die like that? He could have let a dam break in any number of other communities where there were a bunch of drunks and no-goods. Why didn't he do that?"

I said, "Eric, if God would have allowed a dam-break among those other people, where do you think they would have gone when they died?"

Eric said, "I guess they would have gone to Hell."

I asked him, "What about the ones that died at Toccoa?"

He said, "I guess they went to Heaven"

"So, Eric," I asked, "Which kind of God would be more gracious and loving: a God who would allow thirty-nine no-goods as you call them, to go to hell or a God who would take thirty-nine of His children home?"

As he paused to consider that, I think Eric realized how bad it would have been for thirty-nine unsaved, non-Christians to have been killed instead of the saved ones who had died. Eric also saw how important it was to have a relationship with Christ. So he accepted Jesus as his Savior; now that's a changed life!

## THE AFTER YEARS

Since the dam-break, many of my thirteen brothers and sisters have come to that same place of decision in their lives. October 12, 1980, I had the wonderful privilege of leading my Mom to the Lord. My mother died at the age of ninety-eight but she was seventy-one years old when she became a Christian. She walked with the Lord twenty-eight years before passing away on April 25, 2008.

I asked her often, "Mom, are you sure you're saved?" She would give me the biggest smile, and her eyes would sparkle, and she would say, "Yes, I'm sure I'm saved and going to heaven." What peace that always gave me. Just think about it. Mom is already in heavenly places with Christ, Jesus.

Ernie, Sam, Ronnie, Bud, Big Chat, Bill and many others of my family have found that "peace which passes all understanding" as they have turned their lives over to Jesus Christ as Lord, Savior, and protector. He is the forgiver of sins, the one who gives peace here and now, and the giver of eternal life in heaven in His presence.

No, the bitter waters have not become sweet, but because so many lives have been touched by the witness of survivors, the memories have become bearable. The stench of it all is finally gone. In its place I see many young lives being prepared to walk the path we have left behind for them to follow as they come to be educated and then sent out into the world with the message of God's love for the World.

I, too, have that inner peace with God, but I have to admit that I still struggle at times. When I do, I turn to God who is my comfort, who promises me that if I never find complete peace here, it's waiting for me in heaven. There I'll see my precious daughter Jaimée once again. And she'll probably be in His arms, stroking His beard, saying, "Zeezus"

My daughter Jaimée never got to live the life she should have had. My life and the lives of my three surviving children, plus the lives of the two daughters we had after the dam-break, have been emotionally affected too, but we're still surviving and going forward.

## A TRIP BACK TO THE VALLEY

As I sit here writing, today is once again November 6 but the year is 2015, and I have yet a long way to go to find absolute peace about that night of so long ago; that night which is still my yesterday. I'm still working on learning more of what forgiveness of others really means. I know it means my forgiving those who should be held responsible for November 6th, 1977, so I hope this trip will help me come to a place of greater personal healing, emotional healing, and sincere forgiveness toward those who were in charge of the college at that time. As once more I visit my daughter's grave, I will have to face my past and its memories all over again.

## REMEMBERING THE DAY

Looking back now, finally the day came for me to do exactly that: face the memories which still burned deep within me with wounds that would probably be with me forever. From highway 17, I turned left onto the old farm road, drove to the small bridge and crossed the creek. There was where my home used to be. But now it was different.

I was filled with a reluctance to face the past, never-the-less I parked my car on what once was the driveway, years before. As I stepped out onto the ground I remembered the days I had spent in that very same spot with hope and anticipation in my heart.

Now instead of anticipation I felt a cool loneliness come over me. I realized that unlike some other places of my past--places I enjoyed--this one left me with a sad emptiness, just like the plot of ground where my house once stood and where happy days once had been: days when I had cut the grass in the very place I was now parked; days I spent playing with my children as I delighted in their beautiful laughter that bounced through the air--knowing all was well and life was good.

In those days, I had no way of knowing they would be the last days for my young daughter, who taken away long before her time.

Those days were changed in that one terrifying moment that wrapped in that horrible stealth of darkness, unleashing millions of gallons of water from its earthen dam far above, tearing through this very place where I stood, crushing in over us at 55 feet high, ripping apart everything in its path.

Those days and years were taken away from so many of us, long before our time was meant to end, where the blood of many would now be forever mingled in the soft musical rippling of the stream which on that night had screamed upon us taking everything its watery arms could reach, sweeping it away in a wild roar of unstoppable destruction.

Those days would now forever hear weeping from the ground, which would never again be dry. Not because the water of that night had covered it but because it is soaked with the tears shed from the eyes of us who once again stand here and remember; tears that will never dry.

Now the whispers from the breath of 39 lives will forever be heard in the breeze as it rustles the leaves of standing trees which on that night bent and bowed to the maniacal strength of uncontrolled nature gone wild.

## AND I CRIED

As I stood there on this same grass I had once tended to--a well groomed lawn my children played on--now the rapture of that peace was gone. I felt my heart quietly thumping as the blood pumped through my temples and it seemed as though I felt the heartbeat of 39 lives pulsing up through the soil, through the bones and sinews of my feet and legs, as it coursed upward, touching my heart, mingling it's own life with mine, massaging my lonely troubled soul, reaching out to me from the past where those 39 now rested.

And I cried.

For many, the years have passed and have all but erased the memories of that night. But for us who were there and survived, it will never pass away.

That's why we cry.

And for the students of today and of the tomorrow's yet to come, I hope they'll find a new valley of hope, in the place I found to be, the Valley of Death.

## POST SCRIPT

Three of the twelve students we took to Toccoa Falls College from our church in Gibson, Georgia, have been accepted. Because of their academic excellence, two of them have received scholarships. This Sunday we're going to hear one of them preach his first message. He is only sixteen years old. What a blessing he is and will be as his future unfolds.

# EPILOGUE

The church today should be delivering a new message. Not truly a new message, but rather, the old message needs to be delivered anew! It was given to us long ago in God's word, but it has been laid aside and forgotten by many. Some have even walked upon it or have thrown it away. But this wonderful message is seriously needed for the troubled times we are living in today.

There are no other good answers. The troubles in these first ten or fifteen years of the twenty-first century are literally tearing the fabric of Christianity to shreds, while the Church sits in near silence watching it happen, doing nothing. We--the church of today--are complacent as we walk this earthly valley. We have lost our compassion toward those who walk beside us, looking for answers. We have stopped telling the world that there's a Valley of Peace that God has given us. Because of our lack of concern, the Shadow of Death hangs over them, pulling many into the darkness, because they don't know they have a Savior to turn to. And it's our fault.

Every Christian in the church body today needs to be sharing, giving, and standing for the truth. This journey will build and sustain hope for the world. But it starts by spending private time with God each day, and earnestly seeking answers to the following two questions. "What do You want me to do. Lord? Will you please help me do it." His answer to the second question will always be "Yes".

We should not let fear stop us from sharing the message that will change the hearts and lives of others. Fearing they will die without forgiveness of their sins is a far greater fear than that of lacking confidence. This message is a matter of life and death. People need to hear it and know it for the salvation of their souls.

People need to change the way they think about life, and death, and eternity. Safety for one's soul comes only by accepting God through the shed blood of Jesus Christ. No one knows when their last day on earth will be. No one knows when God will say, "Your time is up." People need to know the hope of heaven is real and true. And we need to deliver this message with conviction from our own belief that Christ is the only Savior of the world, and He is the only way to an eternal heaven.

Walking in a Valley of Death will only lead a person deeper into a place of being lost eternally. When this life is over there will be no way out. We have to tell them we, too, have been in that valley, trapped by darkness. Then someone shared God's glorious truth with us. Now we need to share the light of Jesus Christ with them.

How are we going to do that? Well, we can never do it in our own strength. Our strength and courage must come from God. But doing our part means to make a conscious decision to dedicate ourselves to God in a new and fresh way each day. We need to meditate on His Word, pray, and even start a journal of remembrances, showing how real hope based on God's Word can change lives.

As families and the world around them change, people will find the hope they're looking for to abandon the Valley of Death and their desperate attempt at trying to survive there while  miserably failing.

Bill, Peggy, Robby, Kirstin, and Kenny Ehrensberger along with 34 others walked the Valley of Death that night, losing their mortal lives in the frigid, raging waters. But that once peaceful creek emanating from the falls turned into an ugly torrent of death. The violence of the waters swept them into eternity, and brought them to the portals of heaven to be welcomed by God into an eternity of peace. Others of us still walk a valley--a living hell if you will--struggling to survive in the aftermath.

I heard reports that Bill and Peggy's son, Tommy, the lone survivor of his family, lived in a survivors hell for many years. I'm sure the pain of losing his immediate family was greater than the pain I suffered. I hope and pray he has grown from that once confused eight or nine-year-old boy, who rightfully expressed his anger, into a confident man. I hope he's found the Lord's strength to deal with that anger. It's a prayer on the lips of all the survivors because we all still live with some of that anguish and pain.

Perhaps even the President of the College, who was not on the campus that night, also has his own particular suffering to deal with. I hope he has managed to come to that place where God has applied healing to him, so he can have the peace necessary to take away his personal nightmares of that awful tragedy that happened under his watch-care.

Many lives went through the valley that night and were washed down stream. They came out alive but their lives changed forever. Some have been so changed that they'll have to deal with those changes until they draw their last breath. Through emotions such denial, many wish it had been a bad dream one could wake up from. But the truth is, all of us are definitely and permanently changed.

Thirty-nine souls found their end. We once thought it was the Valley of Peace, but it became a Valley of Death; each one came out at the other end into eternity. Each of us will have to travel that same path one day.

## PSALM 23: A PSALM OF DAVID

Most people are very familiar with the twenty-third Psalm, (KJV). I've included it below. While the Psalm has only six verses, they do an excellent job of describing this path. I'd like to start with the last three verses, which are:

*4 Yea, though I walk through the valley of the shadow of death, I will fear no evil: for thou art with me; thy rod and thy staff they comfort me.*
*5 Thou preparest a table before me in the presence of mine enemies: thou anointest my head with oil; my cup runneth over.*
*6 Surely goodness and mercy shall follow me all the days of my life: and I will dwell in the house of the LORD for ever.*

These are the promises God has spoken to us, telling us how we'll be comforted if we are sure we have His Son, Jesus Christ as our Lord, Savior, and Comforter.

The first three verses tell why we have the assurance of the last three verses. That assurance comes only because He is the Lord of our life.

*1 The LORD is my shepherd; I shall not want.*
*2 He maketh me to lie down in green pastures: he leadeth me beside the still waters.*
*3 He restoreth my soul: he leadeth me in the paths of righteousness for his name's sake.*

We all have valleys we walk through in our life but it's the final one that's most important. That's either the valley that leads to eternal life or the valley that leads to eternal death. The question I want to leave you with is this: "When you go through that valley, and you come out at the other end, where will you be?"

# HOW TO BECOME A CHRISTIAN

God has always wanted to have a personal relationship with you, even before He created you.  He chose to show His love toward you, through His sacrifice on the cross, and through His Word.

Here are some very simple steps to understanding salvation and becoming a Christian believer. It's as easy as ABC.

## ADMIT to God that you are a sinner.

Denying our state of sinfulness is like saying we have no need of salvation. But the fact is, everyone sins. We need to understand this, before we can go any further.

## BELIEVE Jesus paid for your sins on the cross.

When Jesus died on the cross and rose again, He paid the full penalty for your sins and mine. And He did it because He loves us, and because we couldn't pay for our sins through our own efforts.

## CONFESS your faith in Jesus Christ.

Share your experience with the people in your life or with anyone willing to listen so they may come to know Him too. Talking about it proves you believe it.

### Romans 10:9-10
*"If you confess with your mouth that
Jesus is Lord, and believe in your heart
that God raised Jesus from the dead,
you shall be saved; for with the heart
man believes unto righteousness, and with the mouth
confession is made unto salvation."*

## *Take This Step Now*
## THE SINNER'S PRAYER

*"Dear God, I know that I have sinned
and deserve punishment. But because you
love me so much, you sent your only Son,
Jesus Christ, to take the punishment
that I deserve.
With your help, I place my faith and trust
in You as my Savior and Lord.
Please forgive me
and come into my heart.
With your help, I will live for you
from this day forward.
Thank You for saving me, and for
the gift of eternal life!
In Jesus' name I pray, Amen!"*


\* \* \* \* \* \* \*


## Also, as a Christian believer,
## remember to do the following:
1. Read your Bible daily
2. Pray to the Lord daily
3. Find and attend a local Bible believing church

## YOUR OPINION COUNTS!

If you have enjoyed this book,
please consider
**writing a short book review
at Amazon.com**
Help us spread the word,
and share Jesus with others too!

www.ingramcontent.com/pod-product-compliance
Lightning Source LLC
Chambersburg PA
CBHW031324040426
42443CB00005B/209